Art
in Sweden

Leaving the
empty cube

Contemporary
Swedish art

Sören Engblom
SVENSKA INSTITUTET

SÖREN ENGBLOM, *born in 1950, studied art, drama, music and literature at Stockholm University in the 1970s, and was active as an art and music critic with the evening newspaper Expressen during the 1980s. Since 1990 he has been a curator at the Moderna Museet in Stockholm, where he is responsible for exhibitions showcasing mainly Swedish art.*

In addition to articles in the press, essays in various cultural magazines and chronicles in yearbooks, Sören Engblom has written a general survey of Swedish art in the 1980s—From Interspaces and Broken Metaphors—as well as monographs on the artists Rune Jansson and KG Nilsson.

© 1998 and 2002 Sören Engblom and the Swedish Institute

2nd revised edition 2002

The author alone is responsible for the opinions expressed in this publication.

Translated by Hugh Rodwell

Graphic design by Linn Fleisher, cover design by Mats Hedman

Edited by Kristiina Sepänmaa and Harriet Lindh

Printed in Sweden by Westerås Media Tryck AB, Västerås, 2002

ISBN 91-520-0723-5

Contents

Art in Sweden–recent decades

It has been said that the 1980s started with Picasso and ended with Duchamp and that is no unreasonable view. Art has moved from painting, image and form in silence to ideas and objects and events. Art is moving, and making itself heard. Still thriving in the early years of the decade was a largely undisturbed conception of art with its roots in the ideas of the turn of the century. Art worked with colour, shape and the observation of external reality. There were political motifs, expressionist ideologies of persuasion and meditative spirituality. There was art that stayed within "art", and there was art that wished to "reach out."

It is true that art had initiated great changes with the 1960s. The theoretical superiority of the abstract was at an end. A new realism and a new figurative approach had taken over, with their focus on the mass image and industrial production. In the period of transition there was a lot of debate about "open art"—were there really no bounds to what art could look like? Nonetheless everything still seemed the same in the early 1980s, as if the deeper changes aspired to by the 1960s had not taken place.

In the cultural life of Sweden the 1970s were harshly polarized. Pop culture was extremely superficial while political art, theatre and literature were cultivated in pure form. There was also a poetic style following its own separate path. The 1980s began with a liberating, thoroughly permissive attitude that lasted some five or six years. Then a new controversy arose. Old contentions were dug up, and sleeping dogs were woken and started snarling again. In 1987, the critic Lars O Ericsson wrote two masterly articles in defence of contemporary art. They were a reaction to the many unfavourable comments on contemporary art which had been made by older critics over a period of time. And now the debate, which had previously been rumbling under the surface of the art world, broke through into the open.

It is true that postmodernism—an elastically comprehensive term in the context of this discussion—had been a topic of debate since the middle of the decade. At first it had concerned architecture, and then philosophy, where a farewell to utopian ideas had already been sounded in the mid-1970s by the "new French philosophers" Lévy and Glucksmann. (A violent ideological change of direction that took the wind out of the sails of Marxism and gave Liberalism its triumphant 1980s.) The politicisation, theorization and conceptualisation of art increased steeply from 1987 onwards.

At the turn of the decade, the art pages of the press were writing obituaries of the 1980s, at the same time as the cultural climate grew chillier and chillier and polarity was increasing once more. A couple of years into the 1990s, a new left-wing wave of opinion was an established fact, but it was hardly dominant. The situation remained contradictory. In the field of art, however, this period very clearly bears the stamp of Duchamp—ideas and concepts were constantly being discussed in a debate describing art in very cerebral terms. Sensualism became a rarely used word, but at the same time, the "body" (both human and cultural) was brought into prominence, at first with a theoretical superstructure then later counterposed to theoretical dominance. California took this furthest, producing art with very "low" motifs and a ruthless criticism of the stilted and masculine art of modernism, with its abstract expressionist approach. It has been called "slacker art". A powerful reaction indeed against linguistic theory and other highbrow theoretical discussions. In 1987 the Moderna Museet in Stockholm staged its first exhibition with the intention of illuminating the postmodern aspect of art under the title of *Implosion*. It marked a breakthrough for much new and not least photographically based art.

The economic crisis of the early 1990s claimed a number of art galleries among its victims. Particularly in Malmö in southernmost Sweden, it became clear that the good times were over. Art was not selling as it used to. But without prostituting itself to political ends, a change of stylistic orientation nonetheless took place towards installations, concept art, politics and feminism. And the central idea of "investigation" now took its place alongside "project".

This can be seen in art magazines. In Stockholm in the late 1980s, a product appeared on very thick and glossy paper cheerfully mixing art, philosophy and fashion. The choice of title was ironic: HYPE. In the 1990s such a product would be unthinkable. *Hype* was succeeded by *material*, a low budget fanzine produced by largely the same editorial board, which appeared to have been launched under the device: "This is as posh as you'll get". The promise has been kept and as if to vouch for the internationalisation of art, *material* was, for a time, produced in English; then it was enlarged, published in Swedish and produced with the support of The University College of Arts, Crafts and Design (Konstfack) in Stockholm. *Material* was discontinued in 2000. It has been replaced by *Site*.

The important Stockholm Art Fair met competition from the considerably more informal *Smart Show*, and where the 1980s had their elegant white galleries or dark basements and factories, both settings consisting of silent, empty rooms, art now started to find its way to open locations or intimately social places such as hotels (or why not grocery stores?). Galleries adapted to this, became smaller, and followed art and its newly found interest in social life. If the 1980s had a special interest in some mysterious, half-unknown "downtown", in urban culture, then the 1990s investigated all that lived and moved in the city, the agents of desire and the bearers of social patterns. Where the 1980s discussed "the death of the subject" and only silence and emptiness were left, a new view of the subject has emerged today. Not that people think they have any more control of things, but the limitations on the subject are rather seen to be the result of the overcrowded social scene in the city. Everything relates to everything, to travesty the author August Strindberg.

Near the end of the 1990s the economy was improving once more and stability appeared to have returned to the art

The new Moderna Museet in Stockholm, 1998. Photo: Åke E:son Lindman; courtesy National Property Board.

world. The new ideas found expression in the art schools, and internationalisation became a part of everyday life. This may be seen in the routine way in which artists work alternately in Sweden and abroad, and it is confirmed by the Swedish correspondents of international magazines. Quite certainly, this new order has come to stay.

The format of Sweden's new Moderna Museet (Modern Museum) in Stockholm, inaugurated in February 1998, is unprecedented, and its first management was in the hands of a leading figure of the international museum community, the Englishman David Elliott. (In 2001 he moved on to start up the Mori Museum of Contemporary Art in Tokyo and the Swede Lars Nittve, former director of the Tate Modern in London, became the new director of Moderna Museet). Malmö Art Gallery (Malmö konsthall) was, until quite recently, run by Bera Nordal from Iceland.

NUNSKU (The Swedish Committee for Contemporary Art Exhibitions Abroad), previously the smallest of Sweden's public agencies and a formidable powerhouse for the dissemination of knowledge about many of the artists named in this book in other countries, now forms a part of the Moderna Museet. The relationship of Swedish art to other countries is now self-evident in a completely new way.

"Everyday life" has been a constant theme in the most recent ten-year period. In addition, there is a whole spectrum of ecology, politics and feminism. But the grand style, sublimity and poetic delicacy are all far from the centre of artistic life today. Artists have an unflinchingly unheroic relationship with objects, cameras, earth, animals and plants. Film—which very often means Hollywood film—seems to be the most powerful medium of our time. However (popular) music also means a lot to artists as well as to almost every young person today. Consequently, a wave of sound (or noise) art is rolling in, alongside videos and installations, which in their turn often contain sound as a basic element of expression. Art in general is showing great interest in the new Eastern and Central Europe which has been opening up after the fall of the Berlin Wall in November 1989.

But there are reports from the art schools of a newly-awakened interest in painting—can this be true? Of course it can. Actually, the signs are already showing in the galleries. In the spring of '98, the art magazine *material* devoted a very long essay to the question of a new concept for painting. The rumours of the death of painting are probably just as exaggerated as they always have been, just as similar rumours of the death of the novel usually are. And recently, deeply existential subjects seem to be finding their way back into contemporary art. Art keeps shedding its skin, perhaps a little more often and a little more rapidly than before, but a look at the artists in the display rooms shows that creativity still thrives. It is a fact that there are more and more artists. The fine arts programmes at Swedish upper secondary schools are swamped by students, as are the media programmes. More young artists than ever before are graduating from art colleges. Both numbers and mobility are increasing. The future of art depends on how it will be able to handle its new conditions of existence.

The artists in the rooms

In October 1996, the exhibition *På: Tiden* (On/About Time) opened at the Moderna Museet in Stockholm. Its subject was about contemporary Swedish art and there were 21 exhibitors. Two exhibitors were groups, making 26 artists in all—a mixed collection of 11 women and 15 men, most of them born between 1957 and 1968. The techniques vary from painting to sculpture, drawing, installation, photography, film, video and multimedia. There are silent rooms and rooms full of noise.

Bengt Olof Johansson. "Brännkyrkagatan 54 A". From On/About Time, 1996.
Photo: P-A Allsten, Moderna Museet.

Cover recordings of Abba may be heard in one corner, while the actor Gösta Ekman is quietly but intensely reading a text at the other end of the industrial basilica of the tram depot (the temporary exhibition area of the Moderna Museet while its new home was being built). Dresses spin and subside into handbasins, voices buzz around a dinner table, water runs in a darkroom that is also a kitchen, while very close by there are computers to process, video films to be seen and photographs of contemporary Swedes, from the refugee centre in the forests of the province of Värmland to the garage in the well-heeled Stockholm suburb of Djursholm. There is introvert art and extrovert art, installations in slow decay and constructions of sudden concentration... It is the third large-scale show of contemporary Swedish art in just one year.

At the Rooseum Center for Contemporary Art in Malmö, eleven artists, five of them women, put their work on display in the exhibition *Se hur det känns* (See how it feels). Compared with the well-filled rooms of the *On/About Time* exhibition, this feels slimmer, but there is the same absence of any general theme as at the Moderna Museet. On the contrary, the exhibition's organizer, Rooseum director Bo Nilsson (currently the director of Liljevalch's Art Gallery in Stockholm), declared that the exhibition could be seen as eleven separate exhibitions covering sculpture, painting, installation, drawing, video and performance arts. But neither is technique any real key to sorting out impressions of the exhibition, he added. Just the opposite in fact: "Artists choose the medium that is appropriate to the work of art they are producing, which sometimes leads them to transcend boundaries and create interesting cross-fertilizations". As with *On/About Time*, many of the artists were working abroad, often on temporary grants, but some more or less permanently. Three of the eleven artists at the Rooseum were also exhibited at the Moderna Museet exhibition.

The third survey of 1996 was more comprehensive, with more older artists represented and an even more motley mixture of styles. But neither was *Alone together* (original title in English), at the Liljevalch's Art Gallery in Stockholm, a thematic exhibition, as in fact the title tells us. Visitors had to reach their own general conclusions, and that was no straightforward task with 37 exhibitors (20 male and 17 female) showing their work. But with such breadth much of contemporary Swedish art was on display, including art outside the fashionable trends of the moment, although none of the artists at Liljevalch's were strangers to the informed public. Painting, sculpture and objects, both still and moving, dominated *Alone together*, but photography was also represented.

The exhibition catalogue compared Swedish artists to trees in a forest, each standing tall in its own spot, but nonetheless all belonging together in the same forest, even if it might be difficult for an individual observer to see the connexions. Historians and critics often wish to bundle players together according to certain lines of development, but: "the real trees, standing powerfully alone, pay little attention to this". This sounds like an echo from the distant past, given the markedly social character of young contemporary art. But of course the remark is apt—anyone attempting to sketch an image of their own period must reach conclusions by reducing the variety confronting them.

Taking these three exhibitions as a starting point, it is possible to provide an overview of the past ten years and also follow a number of threads further into the past. It cannot be completely impartial—the text seeks out certain tendencies that are new or at least typical of the period. For this reason many older artists will not be included in this survey. These three exhibitions do not give any complete picture of what is happening in Swedish art at the end of the twentieth century, of course. A partial truth is provided, one that moreover depends to a certain extent on media coverage of art. (And we may well ask who or what decides which art is most visible—is it the public, the media, the art institutions and galleries, or even the artists themselves?)

These three exhibitions were organized by curators wishing to maintain a low profile so that the art would be more visible than the exhibition concept. This attitude would appear to go against current trends as they are presented in contemporary critical texts. Although art museums have a century-long tradition of thematic exhibitions, the term curator had to be imported in the mid-1980s to designate an organizer who steers more actively and is more visible than before. The reluctance of institutions to thematize and classify may be seen as a counterweight to other forces governing art outside the studio. However, museums and art galleries are powerful players in the art world because of the significance of the selections they make. Many of the most important artists were not represented in these exhibitions and for this reason I shall undertake numerous excursions. But the participants represent most of the orientations and tendencies that typify the contemporary art scene and allow us to draw a number of plausible conclusions that will be pointed out in due course.

Lena Cronqvist. "Hand i hand I"
(Hand in hand I), 1993-94.
Courtesy Galleri Lars Bohman.

An expressive line

A very Swedish tradition in painting has been given the label expressionist, although it owes little to German painting of the *Die Brücke* school. In the modern history of Swedish painting such artists as C.F. Hill, August Strindberg, Ivan Aguéli, Bror Hjorth, Vera Nilsson, Sven X:et Erixson and Hans Viksten have all followed this line. Today artists such as Karin Mamma Andersson (b. 1962) continue the tradition in their own personal way, but this expressive, committed, figurative style of painting also provides a resonating ground for other painting in Sweden today. Lena Cronqvist (b. 1938) made her debut in the 1960s, but was not attracted by such fashionable styles as pop art or photographic realism. Her painting, full of social and existential empathy, steers the problematic of the everyday over towards the great tragic questions. Her art was most in tune with the times in the 1970s, a period when social commitment and political agitation in certain areas of Swedish art was practically considered compulsory. She has moved on, however, by way of such work as a suite of paintings on the dance theatre of the German choreographer Pina Bausch. She has extended her range to include sculpture, producing small, black pieces that have surprised and impressed observers. Foreign critics have been particularly attentive, and Lena Cronqvist is as much written about today as she ever has been. The idiosyncratic Rita Lundquist (b. 1953) is also working within this tradition of Swedish 20th century art, displaying strict loyalty towards her *leitmotif*, a lonely girl in a cold environment.

A provocative picture of the state of affairs in the Swedish welfare state in the late 1960s and particularly the 1970s was painted by Marie-Louise Ekman (b. 1944). But like painter and artistic allrounder Carl-Johan De Geer (her former husband) she has always worked in parallel with film, producing works like *Hello Baby* in 1976 and *Barnförbjudet* (The Elephant Walk) in 1979. During her professorship at the Royal University College of Fine Arts in Stockholm she became an important source of inspiration for many of her students. In 1999 she became the head of this college, following the painter Olle Kåks. She was also responsible for the television series *Målarskolan* (Learning to paint), which missed no opportunity of poking fun at antiquated views of art and artists. This was symptomatic in its foresight as the art world of the 1990s has not the slightest inclination to see artists as romantic heroes. And film is the medium which currently seems to mean most to young artists. Julian Schnabel, Robert Longo and Cindy Sherman may be numbered among leading international artists of the 1980s now working with film.

But painting is not the first art form that comes to mind when considering artistic expression in contemporary Sweden (even though a new wave seems to be approaching). In *On/About Time*, for instance, installations were predominant. At the Rooseum, however, Sophie Tottie (b. 1964) showed a more modern way of using painting as an appropriate adjunct to the work of art involved. Tottie, who now lives and works in Stockholm and Berlin, but used to work in New York, has for some years been developing a "stripey" black and white style of painting which might well recall the work of the American painter Agnes Martin. She has transcended this minimalism, however, and using a heavy rule and violently applied colour she has created what might be described as an encounter between minimalism and action painting. For her, it is not primarily a question of stylistic confrontation, but rather of charging the impeccable regularity of the lines with an anxiety alien to it. In parallel, she displayed photographs of public environments with functionalist furnishings (whose repetitive formal language takes up the theme of rectilinearity) and a video in which we encounter a terrorist. It is a kind of rewriting of history in which apparently innocent forms are shown to brood on concealed and disagreeable foundations.

Cecilia Edefalk (b. 1954) may also be perceived as repetitive in her choice and presentation of motifs, but at the same time more delicately painterly (and yet hard-boiled). She used to

Sophie Tottie. "Abandonado", 1997. Indian ink, plexiglass.
Photo: Elio Montanari; courtesy andréhn-schiptjenko.

Cecilia Edefalk. "Echo", 1993-94. Oil on canvas. Photo: Ulrich Littkemann.

live in Bremen, in Germany, and has been more active on the Continent than in Sweden. She also has first-hand experience of the mass media, as she was originally a graphic designer and illustrator on television. A fundamental experience for her was the realization that the television news was a reality in itself to such a great extent, governed by the special demands and needs of the medium. She found this sick. Her painting often contains, possibly as a result of this insight, a tension between the authentic and media reproduction. The repetition of a motif in her work forces viewers to slow their pace of observation. By seeking out the at first almost invisible variation, an observer becomes aware of the image in such a way that in spite of its figurative motifs it is able to display abstract qualities. Edefalk used this approach in an early work, *En annan rörelse* (Another movement), a series of paintings of various sizes of an advertising image for a suntan lotion. The man is applying it to the woman's back. But the bottle itself, the product, is missing. In this way of course, the significance of the picture becomes enigmatic and provocative to the viewer. An erotic atmosphere is conjured up, but no clear signs are available to pin it down.

More recently one of her interests has been working with self-portraits repeated along the walls. At the Rooseum, the room and particularly the floor had a grey colour that was close to the dominant grey of the paintings. A tranquil and very precise installation, although it was only really about hanging paintings in a room. The self-portrait is based on a photograph. "The image of oneself always comes from outside… Paintings on the other hand come from within—they are an attempt to recall something. Photographs in themselves (as a technique) do not interest me…" The first painting becomes the starting point of a slow process: "I produce repetitive series, but I do not want to repeat myself. That's why it takes time". This investigative slowness is a question of *timing*, the nuances in her painting are often a question of the rhythm of the image, of giving the repeated image of oneself something that was not there in the photograph. But—as the catalogue to *See how it feels* points out—this expression, based on emotion and in contrast to the linguistic and intellectual approach of the 1980s, manages to avoid the "expressionist trap". Cecilia Edefalk's repetition has nothing to do with persuasion.

Everyday matters

A long series of self-portraits, executed one every morning and amounting to some 500 or more, has been occupying Carin Ellberg (b. 1959) for a number of years. She maintains, however, that these portraits do not constitute a central project in her work, but they have grown into a touring exhibition by virtue of their lucidity. Her art is directly linked to daily life, even at its most private: children and everyday chores.

Carin Ellberg. "Selfportrait", 1995. Courtesy c/o Atle Gerhardsen,
Oslo and andréhn-schiptjenko.

But Carin Ellberg has an intriguing distance to her work. Her busts of female colleagues are produced in various materials associated with the subject—colourful clothes are shaped into pillars and nylon stockings are formed into decorative intertwining patterns with the help of paste, producing ambivalent associations to bodily fluids... Perhaps, as in *On/About Time*, a small minimalist painting is added, drawing the viewer's attention to a plughole. In her everyday images there are intimate and private references, it is true, but they also tell something of the encounter between life (private and biological) and modernity. In a work based on the life and notes of a social worker at the Museum of Labour in Norrköping, 1993, Ellberg extends herself in a more comprehensive project, towards another person's life and experiences of contemporary Swedish society. Her mid-career retrospective took place during the autumn of 2001 at the Uppsala Art Museum.

For several years now, Swedish art has been replete with the everyday. The trivial, the "low", the familiar and impersonal—from the everyday objects of bathrooms and kitchens to a more far-reaching consideration of what is concealed or left over—this is all an area being explored by both male and female artists. There are meditations on the objects in themselves and a more extrovert interpretation focusing on their environment as a whole. A study of the contemporary situation making use of social and political perspectives evokes a documentary attitude to the subject, while an intensive study of the workings of memory proceeds on another more poetic path. Both approaches may be found in the work of Anders Widoff (b. 1953), but a melancholy study of memory appears to predominate.

In the greyest month of 1993, November, the exhibition *Alla namn* (All names) opened at the Moderna Museet. Anders Widoff transcended certain boundaries in relation to the routines of the museum. He brought out works from the museum collections that are rarely or never shown and displayed them as they are kept on the shelves of the storeroom. He "commented on" or "paid homage to" the big names, especially those of Swedish twentieth century art that were being shown by the museum at the time, using cut flowers— as is the tradition at graduation exhibition openings at art colleges. He also filled a small room with surplus chairs, very anonymous ones, clad with everyday fabrics associated with the recent Swedish past but also perhaps with a certain kind of abstract "modern art". His large square-patterned paintings were placed in close proximity—with patterns at once modernist and powerfully reminiscent of the plastic tablecloths found in thousands of Swedish kitchens twenty or thirty years ago.

Widoff's square patterns are related to the problems he has always experienced interpreting the neoplasticism of Piet Mondrian's work. He has also commented on older art that is still perhaps on display in public places. Art which no-one sees any more, although it's still there. The atmosphere of the past broods over Widoff's work, the tranquil reflection that remains when oblivion has claimed its own. He views abandoned objects with the tenderness of a phenomenologist or a collector, "just as they are". At the same time the optimism of past decades is showcased in his images, just as it is in public furniture or public works of art. It is no pure nostalgia, it is rather a question of focusing attention on what falls by the wayside, whether because it is difficult to classify or quite simply because it is no longer used. He tries to work beyond hierarchies and ideologies, which in his opinion obscure the view in the world of art and particularly in museums. "Fundamentally, art is a subdivision of reality." His painting can be tentative, letting a line of text recall an abandoned location or time that passes—only to stay for ever in the dimly lit recesses of memory—or to be executed with precision after a correspondence course in traditional motifs to see if it is

Anders Widoff. "A Capella", 1993—from the exhibition All names.
Photo: P-A Allsten, Moderna Museet.

Jan Håfström. Triptych from Mr Walker: "Angivaren" (The informer), "På stranden" (On the beach), "Gatan utan namn" (The street without a name), 2001.
Courtesy: Färgfabriken

possible to produce a trivial painting. (The task shows itself to be no easy one.)

Widoff shares his interest in memory and time with an older painter, sculptor, installation artist and (occasionally) critic, Jan Håfström (b. 1937). An inventor, or perhaps rather a discoverer, Håfström does not just go hunting for time that has flown, but also for images that have endured and acquired a warming patina or a deepening reminiscence of conflicts, shortcomings or sheer human tragedy. Signs of this kind were especially evident in his very successful 2000 exhibition *Mr Walker* at Färgfabriken (Center for Contemporary Art and Architecture) in Stockholm.

26

Memory on the terms of oblivion

In the 1960s, Håfström was attracted by the mass image, although no frictionless pop art flowed from his brush. Instead the earth attracted his interest and he took decay, the passing of material things, as his theme. In combination with his focus on the mass image (borrowed from the press and films), including his own strip cartoons and childhood drawings, he gradually evolved a way of reappropriating shadowy experiences. At the same time relentless processes were presented in a dusky twilight of memory that was not however permitted to obscure any unpleasantness.

The form language that interests Håfström is minimalism, his major source of inspiration is the early 1970s in the USA, where he came to know Gordon Matta-Clark and others. He will be remembered for his great figurative paintings from the years around 1970, and for his curiosity as to what could be

Jan Håfström. From "Ibid. II", 1983. Installation. Photo: Sven Åsberg.

found in the USA in the 1970s, a period when the art focus of Swedish media was on a more provincial, explicitly political approach. In 1976, Håfström found a school in the borough of Queens in New York, set up his studio there and thereby initiated a long period of Swedish scholarship visits to America to what became known as PS 1. Here there are both studios and an exhibition hall. On his return to Sweden he got together a group of colleagues, and they sought out the abandoned linseed oil factory in Danviken, an old industrial area on the outskirts of Stockholm's inner city. There were three exhibitions sharing the title *Ibid.* (the Latin abbreviation for at the same place). The artist behind the title was Alf Linder (b. 1944), who also staged *Ibid. III* in Borås. *Ibid. II* took place in a subsequently demolished part of the well-known München brewery complex in Stockholm. The *Ibid.* exhibitions formed a special, rather romantic, almost gothic, orientation for a number of projects in abandoned premises in the 1980s. Such exhibitions are surrounded by silence—lingering significances from the layers of past activities in the abandoned rooms thicken into an atmospheric context that may signal both presence and absence. This silent installation art occupies a special space in the Swedish art of the 1980s that is most closely related to American post-minimalism and earth art (in its urban metamorphoses). At the same time, the style itself of these projects represents a typical aspect of the 1980s, something silent and desolate that transformed itself into a growing social intensity towards the end of the decade, and then in the 1990s grew into a tendency to dwell in rooms full of life rather than ones that have been abandoned. (There will be further reflections on this in the chapter on the locations of art.) By reason of his versatility, Håfström has come to occupy a very individual and wide-reaching position in contemporary Swedish art. His influence may be seen in younger artists like Katrine Helmersson (b. 1958), and an affinity with his work may be found in such artists as Mikael Lundberg (b. 1952).

The painter Ola Billgren (1940–2001) also has his place among the "artists of memory". Like Jan Håfström he first won notoriety in the 1960s with paintings in a style which may be interpreted as Nordic photorealism. But this figurative style of painting, with its extremes of ambience and precision, was actually more rooted in French film and nineteenth century Danish painting. The encounter between this tradition and urban Swedish reality gave the paintings their distinctive character. During the 1980s Billgren affirmed a musical abstractionism (in paintings executed in dialogue with the music of Chopin) which was allowed to fuse with his earlier work. His collages investigated mass-media realities with poetic finesse and became almost emblematic for a period. During the 1990s—once more paralleling Håfström—he had large retrospective exhibitions dedicated to his work at the Rooseum and the Moderna Museet. He progressed to what some wish to regard as a dialogue at a distance with Gerhard Richter in a suite of red paintings, a kind of highly developed defocusing of still life and interior motifs. When Ola Billgren died in the autumn of 2001, a powerful and intelligent master of contemporary Swedish painting took his leave of us.

Billgren took part in *Ibid. II* in the old München brewery in Stockholm in 1983. Håkan Rehnberg (b. 1949) and Johan Scott (b. 1954) belong to the same circle. These are two very individual painters who have staged some important exhibitions together despite their differences. Whereas Rehnberg works in a non-figurative abstract style with certain philosophical starting-points—be it Heraclitus or Maurice Blanchot—and painstaking methodological investigations, involving particularly work with yellow monochromes on matt sheets of perspex (giving the paint a distinctive, transparent tone) in the 1990s, Scott's painting has always been more rooted in instinct

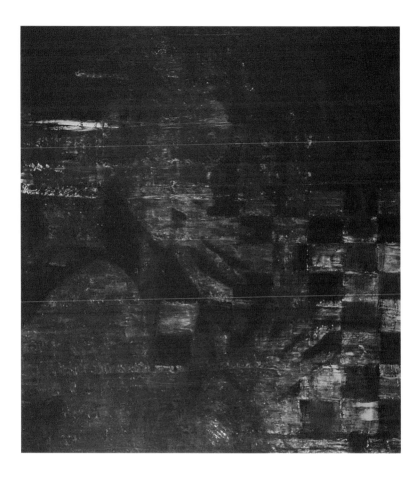

Ola Billgren. "Drömmen" (The dream), 1993. Oil on canvas. Courtesy Galleri
Susanne Ottesen, Köpenhamn.
Håkan Rehnberg. "Utan titel" (No title), 1995. Oil on acrylic glass. Photo: Jan Almerén;
courtesy Galerie Nordenhake. Facing page, top.
Johan Scott. "Utan titel" (No title), 1997. Oil on silver leaf on polyester.
Courtesy Galleri Gunnar Olsson. Facing page, bottom.

and emotion. But since he was originally a student of architecture and consequently has a powerfully structural sense of composition at the foundations of his work, his pictures develop as the decay of an initially strict composition. Combined with strong colours and well-balanced but sharp contrast, Scott's artistic expression retains its charge. The place of the quotations from the history of art in his 1980s paintings has recently been taken by an emphatically subjective approach. The most recent occasion on which Rehnberg and Scott collaborated was the exhibition *Hypotes Ormen* (The Snake Hypothesis) at the Royal Academy of Fine Arts in 1991, one of the most memorable encounters of the 1990s in Swedish painting.

In this connection it is worth mentioning the Swedish tradition of painting in the sublime style. This is an independent—it may be either abstract or figurative—approach to painting with its roots in the turn of the century but also in later expressive art, that effortlessly finds its place in the contemporary Swedish art scene. In the 1980s Torsten Andersson (b. 1926) experienced a great resurgence of interest in his timeless painting with its unique decorative shapes forming a distinctive, almost sculptural world. Jarl Ingvarsson (b. 1954) has continued working on his everyday but powerfully expressive colour poem. The abstract works of Rolf Hansson (b. 1953), which occupy a borderland of abstract expressionism, organic structure and in recent years—quite unexpectedly—a figurative approach of dreamlike memory character in *Huset* (The house), 1994, are still in full development. Ann Edholm (b. 1954) has been working in a powerfully abstract-expressionist style but has more recently discovered a minimalist form-world of signs, as distinct in shape as they are enigmatic in content.

Ann Edholm. "Brottyta (Den nionde timmen)" (Fracture [The ninth hour]),
1996. Oil on canvas. Photo: Jan Almerén; courtesy Galerie Nordenhake.

Out of dark inter-spaces

From the—literal!—earth of the early 1980s, the Wallda group of artists emerged, comprising Eva Löfdahl, Max Book and Stig Sjölund. (They took the name Wallda from the health-food company that was the tenant before them in their studio premises in Årsta in southern Stockholm.) Their first project had the strange and humorous name of *Boplats Otto* (Residence Otto), and consisted of a number of small cabins resembling outdoor toilets garishly painted in modernistic concretist patterns and placed on Årsta Common with high-rise flats and industrial buildings in the background. This was a parody of that year's Swedish home and housing exhibition "Boplats 80" (Residence 80), and by the same token a criticism of what was happening in the Swedish welfare state. The choice of location for the exhibition was significant. Much of the work of Wallda and other Swedish art in the 1980s came to deal with repressed intermediate spaces—a kind of no-man's-land. Initially the style was inspired by artists such as the "wild Germans" with their *heftige Malerei* (violent painting), but it also had elements of punk. From the start Wallda utilized different types of expression: painting, sculpture, installation, dance and performance. Max Book has been continuously committed to a hard version of rock music with the "Skipper Worse" band. The Wallda group never followed a programme, but made sudden appearances, a kind of "sensations", "a form of instant art using all the material and immaterial odds and ends with which we are accustomed to surround ourselves". Eventually Wallda split up and the three artists each came to set their own individual stamp on both the 1980s and the 1990s.

Max Book (b. 1953) has mainly worked with painting and to a lesser extent film. During the 1980s his paintings were characterized by the encounter between a dark, *impasto* use of paint and obscure urban motifs. A landscape could be both

*Max Book. "44 flod" (44 river), 1990-91. Oil, lacquer, acrylic, concrete on
canvas. Courtesy Galleri Engström.*

the stage setting of a drama and its protagonist. Book's distinctive blending of categories such as landscape and décor,
nature and culture, sign and matter illustrates the way in
which he has been seeking a "fissure" in his depictions of reality. "Fissures are caused", he writes, "when various phenomena, expressions and aesthetics, in a word entities of essentially different kinds are given the same focus." The concept of
"fissure" was a central concern throughout the 1980s, alongside discussions about the absence of the subject and the death
of ideologies, the death of grand narratives and the death of
painting. The lack of—or the freedom from—petrified truths
and self-evident structures are among the principal characteristics of the decade. The fall of Communism and the collapse
of the speculative bubble economy at the end of the decade
were a sign that external reality, in "true" postmodernist
fashion, was following the lines of philosophical discourse.

Eva Löfdahl. "Korallöar till trettioåriga kriget" (Coral islands to the Thirty Years' War), 1993. Courtesy Galerie Nordenhake.

Book's media notoriety culminated when his works were placed next to paintings by August Strindberg and the great Gothenburg colourist Carl Kylberg in an exhibition at Liljevalch's Art Gallery in 1992. In the magazine *Månadsjournalen* he was referred to as a "great national painter". He has, until recently, held a professorship at the Royal University College of Fine Arts. And he continues his painting undeterred.

Eva Löfdahl (b. 1953) has gradually come to command an unassailable position as a sculptor in the contemporary Swedish art scene. After leaving Wallda, her work became purer in style and its metaphors became increasingly enigmatic. A table illuminated from below with a poisonous yellow light, in a dark room, was her installation in *Ibid. II* in 1983. Seeing the space under a table as a special kind of *inter-space* (in the sense of a *terra incognita*) may perhaps remind the public of Bruce Nauman, or more recently of Rachel Whiteread—interpreted by way of a child's reading of the situation, as a hiding place from the domination of adults. Löfdahl has however long been working with her own special concept of inter-space, a kind of fissure in totality.

Eva Löfdahl is perhaps the most prominent of a number of Swedish sculptors or makers of objects, often women, whose work may possibly be categorized with the home-made label of postminimal objects of meditation. Recently she has been working with perceptions of space, both as a conceptual starting point and in relation to the physical execution itself. The beholder is confronted with something whose surface appears closed, but which on closer inspection reveals itself to be a passage. She occasionally works with expressions borrowing their form language from familiar products, but their origin is not the important thing. This is rather the shift in significance of the form language of the objects which the artistic process entails. The cycle helmets on plinths pierced by tubes in *Korallöar till trettioåriga kriget* (Coral islands to the Thirty

Years' War), 1993, are calmly distorted, but nonetheless they are still helmets that protect but at the same time let through the gaze of the observer. They float in the room like islands. Yet Eva Löfdahl's titles are hardly descriptive: "For me it is about an aspect of this war that is related to an aspect of this work". The contradictory materiality of the coral and its way of growing into reefs around islands are placed in proximity to "drifting islands" of Swedish soldiers who lingered on the Continent in the later phases of the Thirty Years' War (1618–1648) and "drifted (like islands) across the German landscape", "impossible to stop". Once again a socio-political idea encounters physical form, here as often of an organic character and providing a contrast to the object's industrial origin (the cycle helmet). It is not unusual for her objects to

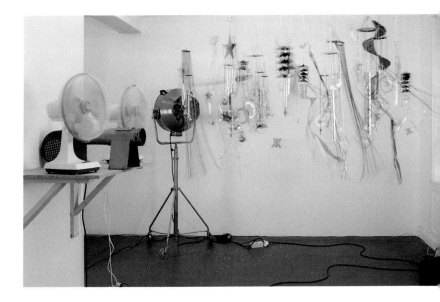

Stig Sjölund. "Handen som gungar vaggan" (The Hand that Rocks the Cradle), 1995. Aeolian bells, fans, tape recorder. Courtesy Galleri Andreas Brändström.

be purely absurd and indeed very humorous—the observer laughs without really knowing why (as in a play by Samuel Beckett). This is especially true of certain untitled works designated *models*.

In 1995 Eva Löfdahl represented Sweden at the Venice Biennale, and in 1996 her work *Sila mygg och svälja kameler* (Straining at gnats and swallowing camels), that had been commissioned by the National Arts Council for the Chemistry Laboratory at the University of Stockholm, was unveiled. In the (modernist) space associated here with a rational tradition for the scientific investigation of a problem, Löfdahl cut a channel to mark out a (postmodernist) fissure in the space instead. The interpretation constitutes one of many possible aspects of the work, which in this context has the advantage of linking this publicly commissioned work with the "sensations" on Årsta Common in Stockholm in 1980 that were so different in their execution.

The third member of the Wallda group, Stig Sjölund (b. 1955), was originally an extremely urban painter. In time he came to work more and more with photographs and objects. In 1991, at Galleri Bohman in Stockholm, he showed a kind of menacing photography alongside neutral everyday objects from the IKEA furniture store—an expression near zero point, a somewhat encapsulated critique of our unthinking relationship to our everyday lives. His later work includes the installation *Handen som gungar vaggan* (The hand that rocks the cradle), inspired by the American thriller. Fluttering streamers are animated by electric fans. Horror and nursery attributes. Kitsch and menace. In the 1990s, Stig Sjölund obtained a professorship at the College of Fine Arts in Umeå in northern Sweden opened in 1987. Thanks to his contacts with artists in Los Angeles he has literally founded a school. "The California style" (with its tension between the mass culture of Hollywood and Disneyland on the one hand and mass murderers and lunatics like Charles Manson and David Koresh on the other) has set its stamp on his work. Artists such as Paul McCarthy, Mike Kelly, Chris Burden and Raymond Pettibon figure in the background. Sjölund belonged to the inner circle organizing the *Ibid.* exhibitions. As a teacher he has established links with the American art considered by many to be the most significant in recent years. The parallel to the *Ibid.* exhibitions and Jan Håfström's efforts to introduce unknown American art to Sweden is evident. There is a clear continuity here—with the possible difference that it's no longer a question of travelling abroad and bringing things back home. There is instead a direct exchange between continents, and this too is typical of the powerful internationalization of Swedish art in the 1990s.

Postminimal/female ...

As early as the 1960s, when minimalism was a novelty, there were artists who, rather than refine the style, form and underlying ideas of the tendency chose to "pollute" its strict purity of form and concept with influences from the opposed artistic camp—abstract expressionism and surrealism. Louise Bourgeois' later work may possibly be considered in the terms of such a blend of styles. This is definitely the case with an almost legendary artist such as Eva Hesse and the American artist Janine Antoni (who has recently been studying and working in Sweden). In Sweden, a remarkable number of mainly female sculptors have presented works in a similar style from the late 1980s and the 1990s.

Annette Senneby (b. 1951), with a lightness of touch akin to dance and a calligrapher's brushstrokes, constitutes something of a special case. In the late 1980s she placed metal sheets on the walls and floor using oil and pigments to colour blue steel. She evokes a sense of weight without volume, a tension between sculpted gesture and gravitation and a sovereign

Annette Senneby. "Utan titel" (No title). Oil and pigment, silver on canvas, 1996.

command of space. More recently she has shown abstract painting with a three-dimensional effect—a tension preserved in the transition from the iron sheets to the lighter instruments of painting. But the gesture retains the expression. In her work the gestures are, as always, stronger than the material, and yet in symbiosis with its weight. You could also say that she spans the opposition between two-dimensional painting and three-dimensional object. A problem which has also exercised Eva Löfdahl.

Katrine Helmersson. "Drömmens navel" (Dream navel), 1994. Fur 27 x 87 cm. Photo: Ebbe Carlsson, Collection Gothenburg Museum of Art.

The encounter between industrial and organic forms, between manipulated everyday objects in enigmatic concentration and images that arise spontaneously—rather than objects representing ideas—are traits shared by many of these sculptors/object-makers. Katrine Helmersson (b. 1958) mentions Bourgeois, Antoni, Robert Gober and Anish Kapoor as her favourite artists in the field of contemporary sculpture. She found her own path by devoting some time to the study of Jan Håfström's melancholy and broken image world. A journey to India deepened her concentration on the spiritual dimension of sculpture that has always been of central importance to her. She frankly admits her powerful interest in the dream worlds of the surrealists, and follows them in celebrating the unconscious. Her work centres on body fragments or other organic shapes, often executed in provocatively tactile materials that invite the viewer to touch them, such as fur, but in sharp contrast to metal. Her objects are sometimes aggressive, sometimes meditative. A sense of presence is central to her work, which has often been perceived as more sexual than it actually is. Her works are rooted in female experience, to be sure—but above all in personal experience.

Charlotte Gyllenhammar (b. 1963) was originally a painter but soon felt that the canvas was like a skin under which infinite possibilities lay concealed. She quite simply felt compelled to move into three-dimensional creation. Her sculptural work is often linked with a process of decomposition. In 1991 she put on an exhibition called *Sprängning* (Explosion) at Galleri Krister Fahl in Stockholm. A doll with the clothes and handbag of a European woman was actually blown to pieces, and then its remains were placed on the floor of the gallery. The title alludes to both an external and an internal explosion. The starting-point is the crime scene, a surface completely occupied by its motifs and dominated by a macabre atmosphere. The effect was shocking, not least for the artist herself, who says she was very relieved when the exhibition was finally over.

Charlotte Gyllenhammar's feeling for space reveals a scenographic aspect of her work. This found expression in a distinctive performance at the Modern Dance Theatre in Stockholm, *Triptych*, in 1994. This was an encounter between dance, choreographed by Margareta Åsberg, and works of art (by Gyllenhammar, Anders Widoff and Dan Wolgers), in which the dancers climbed the walls while the works of art and the audience were on the stage. In *Spelets regler* (The rules of the game), an artists' initiative realized in public places in Stockholm, her space was right in the centre of Stockholm, in the part of Drottninggatan next to the Åhléns department store, and she hung an oak upside down across the street between the buildings. In *Identitet* (Identity) at Galleri Enkehuset in 1992, on the other hand, she exhibited an installation entitled *Brudkista* (The bridal chest), where totality

Charlotte Gyllenhammar. "Dö för dig" (Die for you), 1993. Oak; 120 years old, 12 m long, 10 m wide, 1.6 tons. Photo: Stefan Bohlin; courtesy Galleri Charlotte Lund.

appeared to be on the point of rehabilitation. Her sculptures are not provocations (even if they have the capacity to provoke), but they are about creating an open space for a slow and complex perception. She declares that her works are never about producing the correct answer to any equation: "It's more as if an image suddenly reveals itself".

Charlotte Gyllenhammar's *Olikheten* (The dissimilarity), 1995, is a film that shows the artist calmly working on a head at her workbench in the studio. The projector whirrs and the film is stretched over the head of the viewer, projected on to a mirror and shown on a low tabletop. It is an installation illuminated by the artist's demand for integrity, and at the same time it has a deeply anti-expressionist attitude—the image of the artist reveals nothing about her work, the scene remains a mystery, but a mystery sunk in deep concentration, beyond the reach of the observer.

What happened to beauty? The question is not often put. Nowadays beauty is no fixed norm. There are, however, objects of contemporary art which, without striving for any external beauty in the conventional sense, nevertheless approach a possible concept of beauty for our time with their attitude, their confident approach and their lightness of touch, their sensitive handling of material (with precision of finish but no craft pretensions) and the naturalness of their presence. Reflections of this kind arise spontaneously before the sculptures of Ebba Matz (b. 1963). They can take the form of non-usable furniture—such as a pair of table legs with feminine curves or funnels in the shape of cauliflowers which at the same time form a kind of old-fashioned loudspeakers. The space is filled with lightly skipping forms and inaudible music. The form language is close to minimalism, but the use made of the form and the way it is taken from a known environment (from which the objects are at the same time removed) undermine the rules of minimalism. And the works are not ready-mades, either. Once more we have postmini-malist objects from the hands of a contemporary Swedish female sculptor. In *Alone Together*, Matz exhibited a kind of machine ballet of spinning wooden discs with a white balloon attached to each disc. On the wall there were bells doing gym-nastic exercises with rods which had once borne bell tongues. (It transpires that this is a tender portrait of her ill and aging father, who struggled to the end with the softening-up move-ments of physiotherapy.) In *Kotkas Ros* (The Rose of Kotka) for the *Port of Art* exhibition at Kotka in south-eastern Finland in 1995, a room was filled with outstretched rubber hands, a celebration and portrait of the passions that a legend-ary Finnish tango dancer aroused in the men of the area. Ebba Matz's highly distinctive contribution to the flora of moving

Ebba Matz. Papier maché object on iron stand, 1994. Courtesy Galerie Aronowitsch.

images and objects in the *On/About Time* exhibition at the Moderna Museet was *Vigå*, a small, delicate figure pressed from a tube of silicon, slowly moving between two posts. It is true that her work is often interpreted in readings marked by the preoccupation of the present with sex and identity, and this is often illuminating, but her fundamental concerns appear to be more with universal human themes—always formulated in a remarkably light and confident fashion.

A bed of a simple but sturdy 1950s model, with a lamp on the wall behind it and a chair beside it, stands quiet and still. But the scene is macabre, there is something wrong. Why is the back of the chair made of semi-transparent silicon? And why is the bed waterlogged? The observer sees the worn wilton carpet and feels a chill creeping up his spine. It is like a Hitchcock film, an empty scene anticipating ... The installation *Stol vid säng* (Chair beside bed) was Meta Isæus-Berlin's (b. 1963) contribution to *On/About Time*. She had never before produced such an integrated scene. (It was also shown at *Deposition*, the Swedish Arts Grants Committee's parallel exhibition at the Venice Biennale in 1997.) It reveals the artist's fascination for materials in themselves and for unexpected confrontations between materials. Meta Isæus-Berlin has been working with silicon for a long time, often in a minimalist manner, but obviously a cube of silicon is incapable of just presenting itself as "empty" form. In our day and age it is inescapably charged with an aura of breast implants and similar expressions of a "zeal for improvement". The form is stringent, it is true, but if you touch it, it starts quivering. Another minimal form locked in an expressive battle with gravitation is her *Ballong* (Balloon), a soft container of white, tied to the wall so that gravitation pulls it down. But it resists. Everything in her work is ambivalent, a tranquil process of decomposition. Most of her works are made of materials that guarantee that they won't last for ever—chewy sweets that turn out to be

Meta Isæus-Berlin. "Stol vid säng" (Chair beside bed). From On/About Time, 1996. Photo: P-A Allsten, Moderna Museet.

colourful small dinosaurs threaded like wild strawberries on a blade of grass, but several metres long and hung in a park in Gothenburg in 1995; the gloves along a wall in a work at the Moderna Museet are filled with water and their fingers stretch out over water flowing below them. The gloves must of course be replaced, and the water is an allusion to the *panta rei*— everything flows. The decay of the works does not concern the artist, who rather sets great store by the fact that they resemble life itself in precisely the sense that nothing can hinder their progress towards decay. Total control is not desirable. All flesh is hay. We feel best by going with the flow. Such tran-

Martin Wickström. From "Stunder/Moments", 1993. Courtesy Galleri Engström.

quil wisdom may also be found in the feeling of intimacy that Meta Isæus-Berlin confers on her very different objects in various ways. The materials may be silicon or play dough—both are part of everyday life, both are charged with pleasure and hope, the former in a struggle with time, the latter a greeting from the temporary solutions of the realm of childhood in earnest playfulness. Originally trained as a painter, Meta Isaeus-Berlin recently (2001) reverted to this technique, showing works that relate powerfully to her childhood memories.

... and male

Among those working with objects in a similar fashion a dozen or so other artists might be highlighted, among them Katarina Norling (b. 1963) whose sculpture has powerfully narrative elements, Anne Thulin (b. 1953), Anneli Wallin (b. 1962), Birgitta Silfverhielm (b. 1960) and others. Would the objects be any different if the artists were men?

During the 1980s, Dan Wolgers (b. 1955) produced objects which had their historical roots in both the 1960s and Dada. The objects are reminiscent of Marcel Duchamp, Claes Oldenburg, Jean Tinguely and Carl Fredrik Reuterswärd (b. 1934). But Dan Wolgers is working in a different period and has a special knack of seeking out everyday things and toys or pure kitsch. His objects are all small and often have a narrative character or play singular tricks on the observer, as does *Objekt* (Object), 1981, which is a box with a switch attached. If you operate the switch, the lid opens and a rod comes out and turns the switch back off, whereupon the lid closes once more. His earlier works often have sexual motifs, while his later perspective takes in the whole earth—in diminutive form of course—as in *Objekt* (Object), 1987, a small globe acting as the tongue in a bronze bell whose interior is painted like a starlit night sky. The distinctive feature of Wolgers' art is its humour. But the presence of the humour is only alluded to avoid any of the officiousness that kills all humour. Wolgers is neither ironic nor witty. In the words of Pontus Hultén, former director of the Moderna Museet and an infrequent contributor to books on Swedish artists, he is "friendly and human". His attitude is often very subdued, as in *Objekt* (Object), 1989, 24 photographic objects in riffle technique which the artist himself describes as "comprising twenty-four identical objects mounted in a line, showing a head whose face is turned away from the observer regardless of the angle from which you attempt to view it". This attitude may be found in Wolgers' whole approach to his work, which often deals with the totality of the exhibition situation and gives us reason to take up his work again in the chapter on the locations of art. A mid-career retrospective in 2001 at Liljevalch's Art Gallery in Stockholm provided a comprehensive overview of Wolgers' original and most inventive *œuvre*.

Martin Wickström (b. 1957) also associates to the 1960s in his objects and he has an extremely sensitive relationship to contemporary everyday objects. Wickström is openly fascinated by perhaps the most talked about Swedish artist of the international art scene in recent decades—Öyvind Fahlström (1928–1976). Wickström can be drastically humorous, as in *På fem snabba* (In five ticks) where drawers are shut and opened in an unfathomable random order, as well as dark and melancholy. His installation *Stunder/Moments* at Galleri Engström in 1993–94, which was about a good friend who fell to his death during an attempt to climb κ2, was deeply moving.

Ernst Billgren (b. 1957) is an original painter who seeks a distinctive resistance in his method of working. He investigates the relationship between serious painting and *hötorgskonst* (Haymarket art), a kind of Swedish kitsch at times popular and naive with motifs from nature and at times speculative and prejudiced in its attempts to represent "exotic people". He has no direct contempt for the genre, and in an action with Carl Johan De Geer at Gothenburg's Art Gallery he produced paintings with conveyor belt rapidity. If painting proves too easy—seek resistance in the material. Ernst Billgren turned to mosaic and first of all built picture frames in a decorative style, followed by a mantelpiece for an open fire and then bona fide sculptures such as *Över hela världen* (All around the world) or *Åsikter om andras tankar* (Opinions on other people's thoughts) in this hobby-like style. His motifs are often deer or badgers or some freshwater fish, as in *And landar på gädda* (Duck landing on a pike), and the result is a distinctive blend of pop art and Nordic home decoration, but not in any coolly aesthetic sense related to "more beautiful everyday objects" (the typically cool Nordic style of interior decoration with light wooden furniture and simple, pared-down forms in textiles, glass and porcelain). Just the opposite in fact—his work is about styles that have been kept out of elegant drawing rooms. Billgren's branch of contemporary art is focused on popular culture and it has fine root threads in the Swedish naivism of the 1920s and 1930s. Ernst Billgren also makes films and plays in a band, and in 2000 he started an art magazine called *Konstkatalogen* (The art catalogue).

Another, altogether fiercer, attitude to the culture of Swedish populism is represented by Peter Johansson (b. 1964). Using the idiom of rustic crafts he has tackled national

Ernst Billgren. "Över hela världen" (All around the world), 1990.
Photo: P-A Allsten. Collection Roos/Moderna Museet.

emblems like *falukorv* sausage and the colourful *dalahäst* wooden horses. Using the dreamy holiday title *Schlaraffenland* (land of Cockaigne), he has also exhibited a remarkable sauna and an extensively renovated camper van. His contribution to an exhibition in the German city of Münster in the summer of 2000 gave rise to much controversy. It comprised a small raft on which an archetypal red Swedish country cottage had been placed in which a number of skinheads were living, indulging in a raucous alcoholic binge. With this work Johansson demonstrated that there was a more serious side to his art and its urge to investigate Swedish national symbols, the dream of the Swedish idyll, and Swedish prejudices.

Two object-makers who occupy positions of their own in contemporary Swedish art are Mikael Lundberg (b. 1952) and Truls Melin (b. 1958). They are both sculptors with a weakness for objects which provide the viewer with a specific resistance. But there the likeness ends. Mikael Lundberg moves on the margins of the scientific domain—the second law of thermodynamics, about entropy, is always present in his works—and in the city of Venice. This provides Lundberg with a limited but comprehensive context, and his art—in a remarkable blend with the form language of minimalism—has a notably narrative aspect. He uses many different materials and empathizes with the innate qualities of oil, asphalt, mirror glass and metal. He collects objects from such areas of life as manufacturing and health care. Truls Melin builds his opaque and obscure but familiar objects in wood and plastic, and occasionally in aluminium. A dream of wholeness forms an aura about his work, but with no illusions about achieving stability. A finely-meshed net of theory—acquired during studies at the Royal Danish Academy of Fine Arts in Copenhagen from 1979 to 1984—forms the background to his view of his own role as an artist. Where Lundberg's art is oriented towards chemistry and physics, poetry and history, Melin turns to machines, models and architecture, and through this, possibly, to a retrospective focus on the history of design in the Swedish welfare state.

Surface and reflection

During his years in Venice (1985–1990) Mikael Lundberg made his debut at Ahlner's in Stockholm with a number of works in Venetian mirror glass. This was a bold and daring move, given the seductive beauty of the material. The glass was painted underneath and was cut and scored in ways that harmonized with the material and its reflections. His work with glass of various kinds has since led to a number of "entropy series". These are constructed around scientifically determined number series, but where science falls short, randomness takes over. In the Enkehuset exhibition of 1993, a large number of series was shown on the walls of the old chapel which had originally been built for the widows of the Stockholm bourgeoisie. Later Lundberg made a number of asphalt cubes. These disintegrate during the course of the exhibition, the rapidity depending on the viscosity of the material. With reference to the strict minimalism of the 1960s, this might almost be regarded as a parody. Lundberg, however, is well acquainted with the works and writings of Robert Smithson, who has used whole landscapes as a canvas or surface for his sculptural experiments. (By having a lorry dump asphalt, Smithson once "painted" a sandy slope near Rome.) Entropy belongs to earth art, in which Smithson was the first to use the theory as an aesthetic. Lundberg's roots in postminimal praxis, with minimal form encountering informal (organic) elements, form a constant in his work. There is in addition, however, a certain narrative delight related to the geographical and historical context. So far it has been linked to Venice as a model and a metaphor. There, in the summer of 1997, Mikael Lundberg took part in the Swedish exhibition

Mikael Lundberg. "Platser" (Places), 1996-97. 116 places in New York,
374 photographs, 10 x 15 cm, 3rd edition, No. 1/3.
Photo: Roger Andersson; courtesy Galleri Charlotte Lund.

Truls Melin. "Moln" (Clouds), 1993. Wood, plywood, motor.
Photo: Jan Engsmar.

Deposition (with asphalt cubes, as earlier in the *Balticum* exhibition in Finland, at Galleri Charlotte Lund in Stockholm and at *On/About Time*). He had spent the previous winter in New York on a scholarship. In Stockholm in the autumn of 1997 he showed simple photographs of the places in Manhattan where dossers usually sleep. Nearby he hung small black figures made of paste, like half-decomposed bodies, a commentary on the people missing from the pictures.

Truls Melin grew up in an aesthetically aware environment. Both his mother and his father were designers. He was working with models long before he started his formal art studies.

His starting-points are architecture, engines and models of vehicles: "Everything that can be boarded or started interests me". But it is naturally the exterior of the work that is important—and sculpture as a thing, as something that persists in space by reason of its materiality, with a self-evident presence which continues to spread significance around itself even though the original intentions may have paled over time. He has a very personal relationship to his works, several relate to friends and events in his life. His work at the Nordic pavilion in Venice in 1993 comprised objects structured around a box-like form that was combined with a vehicle such as a car or a locomotive, the whole of which had been covered in glossy monochrome enamel paint—sea-green, red or black. The things become familiar but unknown; natural, but enigmatic by reason of this very naturalness. The paint, deliberately chosen so as not to relate to anything in particular, transforms the objects into images and holds the disparate elements of the sculpture together. A fragile unity is created, in the same way as you might refer to your views being *coloured* by something. The blanket monochromatic painting is related by the artist himself to the *sublime* tradition, and he calls it "shadowing". The whole work is perceived as a kind of elusive tangibility.

Fluxus

The many objects populating contemporary art may be understood against the background of an interest in everyday objects going back to Marcel Duchamp and perhaps also Kurt Schwitters. Both were Dadaists at the end of the first world war and the beginning of the chaotic and turbulent twenties. The art of the 1990s reveals a number of Dadaist elements— perhaps because Dadaism was the least established of all isms. Many Dada objects were also ephemeral in character, as the movement didn't produce its art for eternity. This is an appropriate approach in a time characterized by open borders, the blending of genres and techniques and an ever more comprehensive internationalization of art. Consistently enough, the trend also comprises a newly-awakened interest in the *Fluxus* movement, the most Dadaistic of the artistic currents of the 1960s. A large part of contemporary art is not concerned with objects, but rather with projects or "investigations"—not in the first instance performances in the theatrical sense of the word, but actions carrying on a tradition from the 1960s and early 1970s in the United States. Works by such artists as Elin Wikström, Lars Nilsson and the FA+ group (Ingrid Falk, Gustavo Aguerre & Friends) may be considered as investigative actions of this kind.

"As an artist, I am attracted to movements such as Fluxus and the performance art of the 1960s. Not to silent spirituality," declares Elin Wikström (b. 1965). While studying at the Department of Fine Arts at Göteborg University (Konsthögskolan Valand), she reacted against the orientation of the college and formed a "girls' group". "I found that I didn't want to create yet another thing that would live for ages in a square. I wanted to work consciously with fictive situations, with stories about people." Wikström achieved a kind of breakthrough by doing "nothing", when she spent days lying on a bed at the ICA Malmborg supermarket in Malmö, a stone's throw from the Rooseum. The exhibition, staged in 1993, lasted for three weeks. Eleven artists took part. Wikström created a social situation, spontaneous discussions arose in relation to the (half-) sleeping woman in the supermarket. The title of the work was *What if everybody acted that way?*.

"You might say that in my art I declare war on everything utilitarian, and that the ICA work came into drastic conflict with the normal deliberate consumer activities of the supermarket..." What is involved is in fact a discussion of our way of life, our preconditions and routines. In *See how it feels*, Elin Wikström exhibited a teenager's room with colourful balloons

Elin Wikström. "Hur skulle det gå om alla gjorde så?" (What if everybody acted that way?), 1993, installation. Photo: David Skoog.

The work is accompanied by the following text: "One day I woke up and felt tired, listless, and surly. I pulled the cover over my head, because I didn't want to get up, look around or talk to anybody. Under the cover, I said to myself, I'll lie here just like this, without moving or saying a word, for as long as I like. I won't do anything, just shut my eyes and let my thoughts come and go."

and herself sitting in it, bored stiff. The catalogue compared her work with civil disobedience and referred to John Lennon and Yoko Ono's Bed-in at the Amsterdam Hilton in 1969. "A productive waste of time, as an antidote to rationality and utilitarianism." Another of Wikström's works, *Rebecka väntar på Anna, Anna väntar på Cecilia, Cecilia väntar på Marie* (Rebecka waits for Anna, Anna waits for Cecilia, Cecilia waits for Marie), is associated with Faith Wilding's performance "Waiting" at Womanhouse in Los Angeles in 1973. The theme of that performance was the dependent position of women in society. The waiting of Elin Wikström's women is rather regarded as a sign of trust in a situation of a different kind and more characterized by solidarity. Elin Wikström also used her savings in an exchange action with the public at Galleri Ynglingagatan 1 in Stockholm. Her work breaks patterns and disturbs habits, and makes the public reflect. In the Venice exhibition *Deposition* in 1997, she showed *Oh, shit*, a number of boxes that she moved around the gallery premises. One was very heavy and required help from someone in the public. Elin Wikström signals anti-utilitarianism, but her art is undeniably and deeply functional, the public becomes directly involved. In *Skulptur. Projekte.* (Sculpture. Projects.) in Münster in Germany, 1997, she started a cycle club for "re-cycling" with Anna Brage. In this context "recycling" involved pedalling a cycle in the usual way although it had been modified to move backwards instead of forwards. In *Transpositions*, an exhibition forming part of Moderna Museet's International Programme, which was shown at the South African National Gallery in Cape Town, she told the authentic story of Herr Weimar (whom she met in Münster in 1997) to anyone who would listen; she got to hear a lot of other stories in return. This and other projects involving the public put Elin Wikström in the forefront of the movement of "relational aesthetics" in Sweden.

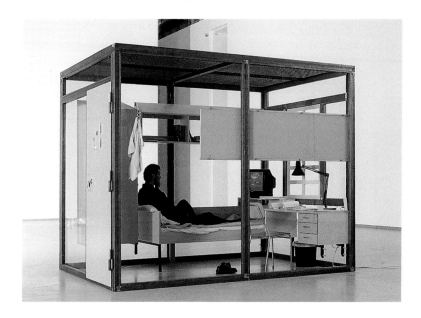

Lars Nilsson. "Gå i fängelse" (Go to jail), 1995. Photo: Jan Engsmar.

Mentioning Lars Nilsson (b. 1956) in this connection only touches on a fraction of his varied approaches to choosing a method of work. In *See how it feels* he showed *Gå i fängelse* (Go to jail). He obtained a prison cell, replacing parts of the walls with glass and adding a TV set, and sat or reclined there for the duration of the exhibition. The TV was on most of the time, and the artist/prisoner quietly greeted passing acquaintances. This seemed to be at the same time both deeply serious—*a prisoner in our midst*—and not serious at all. It was obvious that he was free to leave the cell any time he chose. What's more, he didn't play the part of a prisoner but broke the illusion by reacting when addressed from outside. As in other, very different works of 1990s art (such as Mikael Lundberg's asphalt cubes), Lars Nilsson's *Go to jail* shows a distant affinity with American art of the 1970s, such as that of

Tehching Hsieh. In 1979 this artist had himself locked in a cell in his studio for a year. The intention was a kind of extended meditation, a journey into the artist's soul. During this time, Tehching Hsieh neither watched television, listened to the radio, read, wrote or spoke with anyone outside. This seclusion may be seen as typical of an older, more romantic attitude, indicating a journey into the self to seek one's innermost identity. Nowadays every such movement is rather outward and oriented towards media reality or to openly social encounters.

The performance art of the 1970s had an affinity to the silent rooms of poetry, and very few people actually saw these performances, which were documented in photographs. In contrast, Lars Nilsson in the 1990s gets a lot of exposure—he is displayed at an exhibition and also watches TV, reads and comes and goes as he wishes. In other words, the "normal" everyday context is operating. A movement has taken place from the intimate circles of poetry and silence in an empty room to the media exposure and social chatter of the TV age. Remarkably, the representation and public addressed today is perceived as a collective, in a time of external social individualism, while the individual inner journey of the 1970s was seen by few but undertaken in an artistic community that celebrated the collective as idea and utopia. It is in this ironic context that we observe the movement of art *leaving the empty cube* during the past 15 years.

In Sweden, the performance genre is usually associated with the body as its subject and free dance and mime as its expression and genre. Bogdan Szyber and Carina Reich (both b. 1958) are notable in this connection, with a large number of performances at unusual locations, such as *Beautiful Sadness*, which was performed at a water tower in Hjorthagen on the outskirts of Stockholm in 1989, in which the dancers hung suspended several metres up on the concrete pillars while dusk fell and Laszlo Horvath accompanied the proceedings with sad yet magnificent piano music in a romantic-lugubrious style. Szyber and Reich represent an "impure" avantgarde style with many shock effects and great personal, artistic and financial risks as recurrent ingredients in their work. Humour and abrupt stylistic collisions between expressions of solemnity and elements of popular culture are constant features in this unique mixture of dance, mime, concert and installation. In 2000, Bogdan and Carina carried out the *Millennium Project*. A ritual connected to the city and its history was staged in each of eleven Swedish cities. In Umeå for example, a citizen gave a public talk from the tower of the City Hall. Stockholm did not participate, as another rite had been created here during the European City of Culture Year 1998, but a copper plate at Stockholm Central Railway Station displaying the map of Sweden connected the rites of the eleven cities.

Actions, street theatre and extended, indeed global projects are part of FA+'s method of work. Ingrid Falk (b. 1960 in Stockholm) and Gustavo Aguerre (b. 1953 in Buenos Aires, Argentina) gather around them the various collaborators required by the work they are engaged on: "The Infection Project is an interdisciplinary collaborative project initiated by FA+, in which artists, doctors, researchers, philosophers, semioticians and historians of ideas meet to make a diagnosis of the changeable status of the world around us." *Smitta* (Infection) is partly about the way in which infectious diseases spread globally and the possible chain of cause and effect hidden in this, but it is also infection as a metaphor for the way in which cultures are spread and influence each other, how languages blend and change. In *On/About Time* at the Moderna Museet, FA+—reinforced by Juan Castillo—showed a video from a dinner at the food chain ICA's test kitchen in Stockholm, in which historians of ideas, psychotherapists, image therapists, artists, museum specialists, art historians

Bogdan Szyber och Carina Reich. "Beautiful Sadness", 1989. Performance.
Photo: Anders Thessing.

and others met and discussed infection in a relaxed but creative manner. Four video cameras were mounted above the table and tape recorders bugged the conversation. This all became a room with a white floor covering and white walls in the exhibition, where the edited films were projected on to a long glass table showing hands gesticulating and carrying food and drink to mouths outside the image.

FA+ staged a more aggressive action at a party hosted by the magazine 90-*tal* (The nineties). Here the guests were divided into a cultural elite and a general public, after which the members of the cultural elite had to wait or were driven off because of their status. This was most certainly a shocking experience for some of them. In the *On/About Time* catalogue, FA+ concludes its presentation as follows: "Today you must be fully conscious of the way in which the art game works. First you must have fantastic ideas, and then you must question, harry and criticize them as much as you can. When ideas have got to be carried out you need discipline. We have carried out 17 projects, and it's worked so far. The street is our most important gallery. It's simple, but not easy. It's FA+."

The Dada legacy

As early as what is now known as pre-pop, that is to say the art of Robert Rauschenberg, Jasper Johns or Claes Oldenburg —represented in Sweden by Öyvind Fahlström and Carl Fredrik Reuterswärd—around 1960, the legacy of Dada and particularly of Marcel Duchamp may be clearly seen (which is not to say that Duchamp can only be defined as a Dadaist— on the other hand Dada is a very comprehensive term). As far as the art of the past twenty or thirty years is concerned, the general picture is dominated by the legacy of pop art and minimalism, as was most recently demonstrated in the overview exhibition at the Rooseum *Mer eller mindre—popkonst och minimalism från Louisiana och Moderna Museet* (More or less—pop art and minimalism from Louisiana and the Moderna Museet), 1995.

While pop art got off to a flying start in Sweden thanks to exhibitions like *4 amerikanare* (4 Americans) and *Amerikansk popkonst—106 former av kärlek och förtvivlan* (American pop art—106 forms of love and despair) at the Moderna Museet in 1962 and 1964, minimalism had no launch of comparable impact. In addition, the Swedish art world became more and more provincial in the 1970s, despite exhibitions by important international artists like Joseph Beuys and Öyvind Fahlström; Carl Fredrik Reuterswärd's *Kilroy–Objects and Holograms* and important artists on home ground such as the elegant Carsten Regild and the highly original painter Dick Bengtsson (1936–1987), the media essentially preferred to focus on the theatre and on works of art with an explicitly political orientation and in general on domestic cultural conflicts. When the 1980s, with their more open climate, turned their gaze outwards, the first result was a wave of American art from the 1970s. It is perhaps in this connection that the minimalist or more precisely the post-minimalist breakthrough occurred in Sweden (as described above in relation to Jan Håfström and the *Ibid.* exhibitions). Subsequently, when institutions and media at last began to show an interest in postmodernism, as manifested in Sweden in the *Implosion* exhibition at the Moderna Museet in 1987, a wave of photographically based art made its entry and marked what was probably the most noticeable change in contemporary Swedish art in the past ten years. Cindy Sherman, Barbara Kruger and Sigmar Polke must have made a great impact on their contemporaries, not least on artists working with the camera and photography as their primary instrument. At the same time Sherrie Levine was sharpening the questions relating to the legacy of Marcel Duchamp and the meaning of such terms as "authenticity", "genuineness" and "originality". If we distinguish between the influence of pop and of minimalism, then photographically based art may be seen as the heir to the pop art of the 1960s, while minimalism—especially in its "polluted", postminimal version—may be seen as inspiring the sculptors/object-makers. But it is also quite feasible to mix these impulses—minimalism, too, is rooted in industrial shapes and repetitive series. In Andy Warhol's work both styles already merge in the serial paintings of Marilyn Monroe or even better in the dollar bills arranged by serial numbers or the Coca-Cola bottles.

The form language of minimalism—but almost no minimalism as such!—is as pervasive in contemporary Sweden as the appetite for mass-produced popular culture and photographic images from everyday life. The mixing of high and low has long been such a natural procedure that anyone showing even the slightest of aspirations to conventional solemnity will almost automatically be regarded as an open subversive (in the inner circles of the art world, of course, rather than among a wider public).

Photography, etc.

There is no room in this presentation for a history of Swedish photography. But a quick look at recent decades makes it clear that the pattern follows the general cultural trend, at times even playing a directly leading role in the process of change. The cool objectivity of *die neue Sachlichkeit* in the 1930s took as its model German photographic art, but may be comprehended in the light of the optimism of the Stockholm Exhibition of 1930 (which marked the breakthrough of a new epoch in architecture and design), functionalism and the art of social engineering. The national-romantic period during and immediately after the second world war, which also had German models, was a kind of nostalgia for a time before the evil of the present, while the homage to modernism of the 1950s, with its American inspiration, moved in step with the

Christer Strömholm. "Bleka damen" (The pale lady). Transvestite, Barcelona, 1959/81.

Gunnar Smoliansky. "Stockholm 1978". Collection Moderna Museet.

last successful phase of construction in the utopian political project of the Swedish welfare state. The 1960s entailed revaluation and scrutiny of habits, prejudices and power structures and also saw the exhibition which basically launched photography as an art form in Swedish cultural life. This was the debut exhibition of Christer Strömholm (1918–2002), *Parisbilder* (Parisian Images), at Galleri Observatorium in Stockholm in the early 1960s. His motifs were taken from the transsexual district around Place Blanche. Strömholm was the nestor of Swedish photography, whose centre of gravity was oriented towards artistic intentions. It is conceivable that his significance for the photographic image is similar to that of Ingmar Bergman's for the theatre and cinema in Sweden.

The 1970s were dominated by documentary images. At the end of the 1970s, however, Gunnar Smoliansky (b. 1933) provided a critical and hard-boiled but nonetheless atmospheric analysis of the shortcomings of social development. "Failure becomes a defence of humanism and the dream of perfection becomes its dangerous opposite." The enigmatic and lyrical but by no means ingratiating photographic work of Tuija Lindström (b. 1950) was regarded by Strömholm himself as a continuation of his work in a time of rapidly growing interest in more or less manipulated mass media images. Tuija Lindström, who is now a professor and head of the School of Photography and Film at Göteborg University, also emphasizes that her encounter with the work of Christer Strömholm was quite decisive in her choice of profession. Lindström has produced suites of images both with theatrical arrangements and with a more spontaneous approach aimed at seizing a moment. Despite the classical stringency of her pictures she declares: "For me photography has never been about photography, but about my need to express myself. That this is done by way of a camera is probably accidental. I would not be much good as a ballet dancer or a painter, but the camera is

Dawid (Björn Dawidsson). "#2680",
1987. Toned gelatin silver print.
Collection Moderna Museet.

an instrument I exploit to the full." In these words she underlines the central problem of the photographic medium today. There are opposing views, particularly in colleges, as to the correct path for photography to follow. Artistic liberation, or an instrumentalism applied in the fashion of press photography—one linked to technique and camera-work with roots in 1940s Swedish photography, and the other simply talking about photographically based images freely processed. Tuija Lindström has no doubts about the purpose of professional photographic training. At the college-of-photography level, a three-year programme giving 120 higher education credits (the equivalent of a BA), there is "no sense in learning how to develop film, you must learn how to do research."

Researcher is a title that Dawid (Björn Dawidsson, b. 1949) definitely deserves. He made his debut in the late 1960s after studying at Christer Strömholm's school of photography. In the 1970s he developed a big city style of work with a humorous attitude and a highly-developed sense of detail, frequently revealing a latent streak of surrealism. In the 1980s Dawid produced suites of experimental images using props, recorded on a stripping table or photographic paper, such as *Rost* (Rust), 1983. In his distinctive form of photograms, *Dagrams*, he transforms the room into the body of a camera. He lets the images grow in the encounter between material and light. His images generate a unique gestural world of forms that are unfamiliar

Tuija Lindström. From the exhibition "Järn" (Iron), 1992.

or known from other contexts—bodies and faces emerge from accumulations of objects. Aspects of this work may possibly have links with an older modernist tradition of *objets trouvés* and *objets composés*. Nothing in his artistic orientation would contradict such an interpretation. He has also produced a series of still life images in a dialogue with one of the masters of the genre, the Italian painter Giorgio Morandi. Along with Otmar Thorman (b. 1944), Dawid, Gunnar Smoliansky, Tuija Lindström and Christer Strömholm have finally succeeded in making sure that photography has a room of its own in Swedish art. But the future of photography would appear to be heading in another direction, at least partially.

Photographically based art

At the end of the 1980s a wave of photographically based art started which parallels the postmodern breakthrough (especially in Sweden) and which (in Sweden) is the clearest sign that such a breakthrough actually took place. A number of individual names will serve as examples of this transition. Lars Nilsson has already been mentioned in another context. He was originally a painter who made his debut in 1983 at Galleri Olsson in Stockholm with practically monochrome canvases. A year later his painting was entirely based on photographic images. He used a Hollywood mythology with political undertones—Ronald Reagan and the villa in Beverly Hills which belonged to the unfortunate John Gilbert, the star of the silent movies, whose courting of Greta Garbo was a failure and whose career was destroyed by the coming of sound.

In 1985 Lars Nilsson, whose artistic turning-point was an encounter with Cy Twombly's painting in Paris in 1980, went to New York and deepened his already enthusiastic studies of postmodern aesthetics. The postmodern approach suits him down to the ground as it permits constant changes in style, method and technique. Nilsson emphasizes what he calls "my reluctance to make myself at home in any one aesthetic discourse". During the late 1980s he produced a number of works in a cool grey-white, semi-transparently covering images appropriated from the press. These images may be pornographic pictures from *Hustler*—where the faked orgasm of the models is paralleled by the faked authentic uniqueness of the image/painting—or *The Beauty of Islam*, an elaborate installation using a veiled model. Pointing out an aspect of the contemporary world that causes anxiety and presenting it in such a way that the flow of images from the media is arrested, stripping the appropriated image of its unproblematic "naturalness" and replacing it by something that jumpstarts the interpretative apparatus of the observer—this is a unifying procedure in these paintings from the late 1980s. In this connection he stresses his infatuation with the original image whose significance he has shifted by his appropriation. It is something of a hallmark for Lars Nilsson to be both fascinated by something and to feel anxiously hesitant towards it—and a similar ambivalent experience is probably what most observers will take with them from their encounters with his work. He has since gone on to work in three dimensions, exhibiting the room in which he stayed in New York in the early 1990s or portraying himself as a doll that has been torn to pieces in the bloody manner of Hollywood. He has also created work using texts, as in *Om Makt Dikt och Verklighet* (About Power Poetry and Reality) or combined with video as in *Varför unga män blir nazister* (Why young men become Nazis). Lars Nilsson returns again and again to the deepest causes of anxiety in our time—and yet his presentation is never propagandistic and the collaboration of the observer is required in the spirit of Duchamp that has dominated art since the late 1980s.

Reflections in water

Focusing on a technique is usually rather misleading in contemporary art. Artists tend to choose their technique depending on the needs of the work rather than deepening their knowledge in order to specialize. However, photographically based art had a number of particularly powerful exponents in the late 1980s, such as Fredrik Wretman (b. 1953). He too was originally a painter, and has worked with large images in a cibachrome technique in a purposeful way, extending the technique to fill a whole room in a way that must be regarded as unique in contemporary Swedish art. Cibachrome techniques usually involve strong colours and always have a glossy surface. In this sense there is always a kind of kitsch or commodity aesthetics built into the physical preconditions of this technique. Wretman's approach to working in a room is based on a simple but expansive idea. Pour black water on to the floor, let the water's reflective surface double the extent of the room, and then project a face or a text or even an empty frame on the water, which then becomes a glossy surface with an image (just like a cibachrome photograph).

The culmination of this work is *American Floors*, shown at the Moderna Museet in Stockholm in 1991. During his stay in New York on a PS1 scholarship he spent most of his time walking around taking photographs of famous floors from exhibition locations, mainly museums and especially art galleries. These were developed as large-format cibachromes that were placed on the floor of the eastern gallery of the Moderna Museet. They were in actual fact built into an extra layer of parquet flooring. A minimalist hanging of small photographs representing the same floors was put on the wall, and a reflective water surface was installed at the northern end of the room. Now the public was literally able to go *on* a tour of the exhibits, and could tread the famous floors without actually being there. These medialized images thus granted the access that is so to speak proper to a picture—you remain aloof. That too is the idea behind the reflective water, which may not be walked on either. The edge of the water corresponds to the iconostasis of an Orthodox church. When the Berlin Wall fell, Russia also became more accessible. With the assistance of the Swedish Foreign Office and the museum itself, Wretman obtained 300 pairs of felt slippers from the Hermitage in Leningrad. Wearing these slippers, the public was able to slide over the American floors without scratching the glass above the images. And the exhibition found its full title: *Russian Slippers on American Floors*.

Ingrid Orfali (b. 1952) may be regarded as at least as complex as Fredrik Wretman and far more theoretical. For a few hectic years in the late 1980s, she produced a number of works

Fredrik Wretman. "American Floors", 1991. Photo: P-A Allsten, Moderna Museet.

in cibachrome technique that have no parallels in Sweden for their theoretical edge, conceptual feminism and art-historical symbolism. The mirror image of the observer in the glossy surface becomes a tangible fact—as an observer you are reflected into the work yourself to encounter the contemporary allegories of the artist, constructed in strong colours, preferably red, black and white, and using extremely everyday props such as ornaments, lipstick, tampons, irons and condoms along with such objects as the jaws of a skeleton. Hot issues are handled with icy precision and an extremely intense use of colour, and yet the whole presentation is characterized by analytical distance.

La Chute Ariane—Challenge for Bloody Bastards, 1987, will serve to illustrate the process. Against a glowing red background a rocket falls, made of a tampon and a lipstick mockup. The title is a central aspect of the work. Here, as often, it is given in two languages, with different meanings in each language. Ariane is the name of the (not particularly successful) French space programme—hence the (plunging) rocket. With the tampon as a reminder of the bodily process of expelling blood during menstruation the work is linked to a specifically female set of problems that is physically real and socially complex. In addition there is the myth of Ariadne, the princess of Knossos who rescued the Athenian hero Theseus from the monster of the labyrinth using a thread. The thread is also present, attached to the tampon. Finally, Ariadne is the abandoned heroine.

For a number of years, Ingrid Orfali was the object of a great deal of attention from the art critics, but then she moved to Australia, where after producing one notable work of public art she has not otherwise engaged in any artistic activity.

An objective tone of address

During the late 1980s, the photographically based art of Jan Svenungsson (b. 1961) made its appearance in Stockholm's art galleries. Its dominant motif was a factory chimney which had been photographed and presented in a frame of dark, heavy wood. The photograph thus became a quasi-sculptural object (and the chimney, which on closer observation proved to be

Ingrid Orfali. "La Chute Ariane—Challenge for Bloody Bastards", 1990.
Photo: SKM. Collection Moderna Museet.

Jan Svenungsson. "Det perfekta fotografiet" (The perfect photograph), 1992.
Collection Moderna Museet.

very expressive, became a stoic and at times absurd symbol of the industrial dreams and potency of the twentieth century in a post-industrial age). In the *Rum Mellan Rum* (Rooms in-between Rooms) exhibition at the Moderna Museet in 1992, Svenungsson constructed the first of three realistic and very tall models of the factory chimney. It stuck up from the lawn right next to the museum by the window where Svenungsson had created a closed, guarded and very neutral room for his older, heavily framed photographs. He rounded off his work by photographing it with a large-format camera and producing yet another photograph which was supplied with a text constituting a very neutral commentary. Very subtle indeed is the image he has created by placing his latest chimney—called *Den femte skorstenen* (The Fifth Chimney)—in Motala stream in the heritage area that is the former industrial heart of the city of Norrköping.

Svenungsson is also a consummate draughtsman. In the *Se människan* (Ecce homo) exhibition at Liljevalch's Art Gallery in 1992, his suite of self-portraits was shown. Every drawing took the one before it as its starting-point and distorted it slightly. The technique appeared again at *On/About Time*, where Svenungsson instead chose to show 64 photocopies of drawings of a map of the Nordic countries in which the development shows distortion partly towards the west and partly towards the east. Something which might be a face emerges from the distorted features of the map, and finally only blackness remains. A shaky image of national belonging to which there was a sequel in the form of a number of photographs of the city of Uppsala (where the artist grew up), shown in the *Clean and Sane* exhibition at the Edsvik Foundation in Sollentuna, a northern suburb of Stockholm, in 1997. An objective photographic approach with a simple camera shows a number of functionalist blocks of flats along a street. Precise photographic composition is important to Svenungsson, but the most remarkable things happen in the eye of the observer which suddenly sees the functional *pattern*, the optimistically light facades of this aesthetic, a sudden image of the Swedish welfare state in the middle of architectural photographs in the style of *die neue Sachlichkeit*. And it can only be seen in photographs.

Another, more deconstructed image of this architecture is provided by Bengt Olof Johansson (b. 1959) in his photographs of deserted building sites. They are at the same time an aspiration to build and activity that has ceased. An inter-space. An inter-space that lacks external similarities to those of the Wallda group, it is true, but one that is just as Swedish and just as intensely late in the downward-sloping twentieth century "welfare state" utopia. Subsequently Johansson has worked with digitized photographs, printed on inkjet printers, constructing an architectonic image with these copies in certain existing or created spaces, such as at his exhibition at Schaper & Sundberg in 1995 (and the smaller-scale copy at *On/About Time* at the Moderna Museet, see page 11).

The photographic images of contemporary Swedes created by Anders Kristensson (b. 1958) are quite different and yet they have a point of contact in their objective approach. They are frontal portraits in colour. Eritreans at a refugee centre in the province of Värmland, a family with children at the hypermarket's parking lot, a widow with a Rolls Royce in her garage in the prosperous Stockholm suburb of Djursholm. With sensitivity and a large number of preparatory visits, Kristensson creates a portrait art which at one and the same time presents social facts, opens the image to an anthropological investigation and yet still maintains a personal, empathetic approach towards those being portrayed.

Lars Tunbjörk's (b. 1956) images of Sweden are altogether more drastic. His breakthrough came in 1993 with the photographic suite *Landet utom sig* (Country beside itself).

Anders Kristensson. "Änka med bil, Djursholm, 1993"
(Widow with car, Djursholm, 1993).

Magnus Bärtås. "Neighbour 4, 3 and 6" (installed at Urshult), 1996.

Photo: Carl Johan Eriksson.

The show opened at the Hasselblad Center for photography in Gothenburg and subsequently went on tour in Sweden and abroad.

In the 1990s, photographically based art in Sweden found itself a base in the photographic gallery Index in the Södermalm district of Stockholm. The magazine of the same name with the explanatory by-line "contemporary art and culture" was published by Stiftelsen för visuella studier (the Foundation for Visual Studies) and grew out of the journal of Fotografi Centrum, *Bildtidningen* (Image News). (In 1999 *Index* merged with the Nordic *Siksi* to become NU:, which covers the Nordic area and is published in English). Originally a professional journal, the magazine has gradually extended its scope and in this way reflected a line of development in contemporary art, namely the tendency for artists to select their technique according to "the needs of the work" (to cite Duchamp), not to limit themselves and specialize in one par-

ticular craft. A circle of students from the Academy of Photography at the University College of Arts, Crafts and Design in Stockholm is working with this perspective, and they are not the only ones. Using images from the mass media or other photographically based techniques, they comment on contemporary life by means of combining and shifting given image contents. The magazine *90-tal* (the 1990s) now called *00-tal*—with its centre of gravity in literature rather than art—has played its part in the circle of versatile artists working with the categories of text and manipulated images, both digital and analogue. Those spearheading an art consciously working within the mass media are not numerous. Most of them know each other and form part of Stockholm's cultural colony.

Andreas Gedin. Moscow, Hotel Belgrad 11/6 16.20.
From a journey between Stockholm and Beijing. 1986. Two pairs of quotation
marks were made of lead, one pair was left in Stockholm, the other was
taken on the journey. "My intention was to place the whole extent of my
journey I was to make within these quotation marks." Photo: the artist.

Incorporating the world around us

The distinctive features of these artists include a well-developed theoretical awareness and frequently a thematic approach. They also have an emphatically contextual view of art, confronting Swedish dreams and prejudices, contemporary international ideas and discourses, questions involving the language of text and image and the preconditions of art in particular and human existence in general with empathy and analytical acumen. These artists are versatile, they are able to work as journalists or editors in parallel with their creative activities, or rather they let their observation of the contemporary world take place using a variety of media. Magnus Bärtås (b. 1962) and Andreas Gedin (b. 1958) belong to this group. Bärtås has an original approach to using hand-coloured silver gelatin photographs. His motifs are taken from contemporary Swedish life—renovated houses whose functionalism is preserved in their structure at the same time as it has been transformed in its expression. He has also made a close study of the function and preconditions of memory—in *Bergtagen* (Bewitched) the fading contours of people who had disappeared were depicted by way of their last greetings on postcards, etc. There is a similar modern *vanitas* motif in his candlewax images. Bärtås is also an original writer. In 2001 he published (with Fredrik Ekman) a book of essays, a special mix of modern myths, everyday life and political ideas appearing in the interstices of truths and beliefs, of science and religion. In *Approximativt* (Approximately), published 1995, Andreas Gedin collected works consisting of self-portraits created by using forensic aids which produce phantom images and a computer-generated aging face. It also included a computer-manipulated short story by Hemingway and a photographically documented journey between Stockholm and Beijing, where Gedin first placed a sculpted quotation mark at the starting-point of the journey, and then took a second simi-

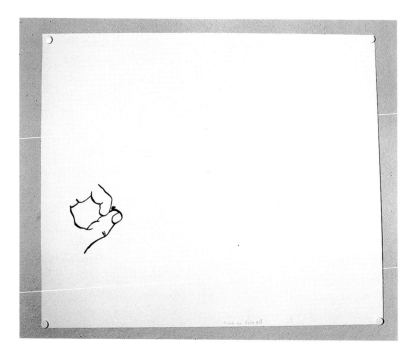

Maria Lindberg. "Time for take off", 1996. Acrylic on paper.
Courtesy andréhn-schiptjenko.

lar sculpture with him on the Trans-Siberian Railway. During
the journey he placed his quotation mark at various stations
along the way, and finally he left it at his destination in
Beijing. "My intention was to place the whole extent of the
journey I was to make within these quotation marks." The
work is in part an investigation into the relationship between
reality and fiction and between language and image, but it is
also simultaneously a way of fragmenting contexts assumed to
be familiar that is at the same time poetic and ironic yet also
sensitive. The manipulated text may recall Dadaistic experiments like Carl Fredrik Reuterswärd's *Prix Nobel,* 1965, in
which the author removed the words from a text by a Nobel

Prize winner and retained the punctuation marks. The quotation mark photographed at so many locations on Gedin's journey is fairly closely related to the works of the Japanese artist On Kawara, in which date signs and postcards from many journeys carry the message "I'm here now". These associations are in no way intended to diminish the originality of Gedin's works. They serve rather to confirm that what is new in contemporary art often entails a tradition of—sometimes openly humorous—linguistic investigations and translation problematics. Gedin has subsequently (1997–98) staged *Viskeleken* (Chinese Whispers) by telephone around the world. A number of people in various countries had two telephone lines open, listened to one receiver and repeated what was said, to the best of their ability, in the other. The texts used were humorous anecdotes relayed sentence by sentence, and all the participants were recorded on video during the 90 minutes of the performance. Gedin is also the editor-in-chief of *M*, the periodical published by the Friends of Moderna Museet.

There are also powerful elements of investigating everyday life and those issues centring on identity as existence that accompany twentieth century men and women on their journey through the growing and global urbanization of existence.

Maria Lindberg (b. 1958) has an everyday and almost brutally humorous streak in her work, which alternates between photographically based techniques, painting and drawing. She is best known for her drawings. Her images are very humorous, often sexually provocative or perhaps just a little sad and direct in their rejection of illusions, as in the everyday loneliness depicted in *Honey, I'm home*, with a girl's head with its nose in the fridge saying hello to a jar of honey. The illustrator Helene Billgren (b. 1952) works in a similar genre, in an equally humorous but rather softer style with a clearer focus on specifically female everyday activities.

Annica Karlsson Rixon. From "Untitled", 1991. Collection Moderna Museet.

Women ... nature?

History, language, gender and identity in image and media are recurrent themes with many of the artists using photographically based techniques. Annica Karlsson Rixon (b. 1962) is an artist who has investigated gender in its cultural context. In some memorable images from 1991 she exposed a shaven female sexual organ in various encounters with a petal and a stamen from an exotic flower, or a chicken with its neck wrung or a flatfish. An eel winds its way between the buttocks

Lotta Antonsson. "Sky is blue", 1990. B/w photo. Photo: the artist.
Courtesy Galleri Axel Mörner.

and up over the back. For male eyes this is both exciting and remote, provocative but with a tender spot that is difficult to pin down. "Culture constructs and is grafted on to the organic. Nature and culture are merged."

The photographed female body, unclothed rather than naked, has in various ways provided a motif in the images created by Lotta Antonsson (b. 1963). But her work is not a matter of imitation or representation, but problematizing and appropriation (that is to say, taking ready-made images from one situation and using them in another). The photographic image as presented by the mass media is our commonest means of communication after words. This means that images are full of signs which make communication possible, but are also slanted and presented on the terms of the dominant media players. Lotta Antonsson takes her images from the media, as with some quietly pornographic pictures of a naked female torso, and adds a text, in this case *This girl has inner beauty*. What takes place? The passive model, the object of the male gaze seeking satisfaction, suddenly assumes an active and contradictory attitude and the observer becomes aware of his voyeuristic behaviour. On another occasion she herself assumes the role of a pin-up, with the challenge *Take it as a man*, which being interpreted means What You See Is What You Get—Nothing More. (An attitude reminiscent of the *cool* aesthetics of minimalism.) In another work she took news pictures from various theatres of war around the world and added texts such as *Skin is tan* or *Sky is blue*. The viewer is inclined to believe that it is the added text which gives the image its absurd or ironic shift, but these texts are in fact instructions accompanying the pictures from the news agencies permitting the picture editors to calibrate their colour scales so that the image will be correctly reproduced in print. That is to say, they are no additions, but elements of reality snapped up by an inquisitive eye capable of seeing what mass media images involve. This sounds familiar. It's exactly the same procedure employed by Marcel Duchamp in 1914 when he takes a bottle drier and puts it in a context in which the public will interpret it as art—and thus become aware of the habits involved in seeing art objects as Art. The photographic image from a mass media context is quite simply a *ready-made*. But in their multiple ambivalence, the photographically based images of our day also take the opportunity of investigating the power structures of the language of the mass media, the preconditions of communication and the prejudices we use to construct our perception of reality.

Two or three exhibitions have been decisive in presenting this kind of art in Sweden. *Lika med—samtida svensk fotografi* (Equals—contemporary Swedish photography) was put on at the Moderna Museet in 1991 in collaboration with the Association of Swedish Professional Photographers *(Svenska fotografernas förbund)* and Fotografi Centrum. It contained a very wide range of photographic images: studies, portraits, advertising images and photographically based art. In 1992, the magazine of Fotografi Centrum, *Index*, produced a more thematically conceived exhibition than *Equals*, that toured the Nordic countries and Europe with the Museum of Photographic Art in Odense in Denmark as its first stop. Around 1990, the magazine had presented the new photographically based art of the USA (whose first major showing was at the *Implosion* exhibition at the Moderna Museet in 1987). At the University College of Arts, Crafts and Design, knowledge of this technique and skill in its use has been thoroughly instilled in the photographers being trained there. In the summer of 1993, fifteen contemporary photographers put their work on show at the *Prospekt* (Prospects) exhibition at the Moderna Museet.

In her suite *Sverige/Schweden*, 1993, Maria Miesenberger (b. 1965) made use of a number of negative prints, all showing

Maria Miesenberger. "Sverige/Schweden", 1993.

Collection Moderna Museet.

familiar, everyday situations. But the figures at the centre of
the images are reduced to black silhouettes, and might there-
fore just as well be perceived as marked vacuums. In an intan-
gible way, the picture feels macabre, particularly when the
image shows a family gathered around a hammock. Are these
black areas wraiths, do they involve an alien presence, or do
they constitute an alien absence in the cult of the present cultivated by the ideology of cosiness and being nice? At
On/About Time, a picture of children on swings was also
included, but an empty swing had so to speak been moved out
into the third dimension of the room, and next to it some
plastic dolls the size of small children were playing. They
lacked heads but had instead something reminiscent of a sexual orifice where their heads would otherwise be. They were
blithely turning somersaults on a pea-green plastic mat.
Recently Maria Miesenberger has been developing techniques

of sculpture and drawing in parallel with her photography. Also at *On/About Time*, Martin Sjöberg (b. 1957) also let his photography grow into an installation. The images were computer-processed print-outs on paper, framed in large rectangles. The motif was a group of racists kicking a black youth to the ground—markedly documentary pictures that Sjöberg had taken some years previously. The images were flanked by IKEA wardrobes and ABBA music (in cover versions by the Australian group *Bjorn again*) came pouring out of loudspeakers in the shape of Bofors cannons. Swedish apples in cardboard boxes and a cosily furry pink rug in the shape of a cartoonist's speech bubbles completed this almost baroque critique of the Swedish welfare state.

Among the young artists primarily working with photographically based art we should finally mention Annika von Hausswolff (b. 1967). In her series *Back to Nature*, 1993, she

Annika von Hausswolff. "Back to Nature" (triptych), 1992.
Courtesy andréhn-schiptjenko.

works in a style resembling police documentation of the site of a crime. Her images show landscapes with naked or half-undressed female bodies, with averted faces and with slightly distorted bodily postures like crime victims. The style is clear and objective in its attitude, although it is provocative in the ambivalence it manifests between documentary photography and deliberately arranged images. Annika von Hausswolf was the Swedish representative at the Nordic Pavillion at the Venice Biennale in 1999.

Near science—and nature

In earlier photographic art there used to be an opposition between so-called documentarists and photographic artists. This is nowadays considered passé, as images with documentary backgrounds have proved able to form part of a presentation in which a new reality is created. In a more long-term perspective this may well be reminiscent of the question that has recurred at regular intervals since the 1960s, concerning the possibility of a meeting between art and science. In itself the question is even older, it is usually traced back to the breaking away by the Renaissance from an art dominated by the power of the church. Leonardo da Vinci is usually held up as the universal genius who saw no frontiers for his inventions—they were just as astonishing on canvas as they were in the workshop. During the 1960s, Billy Klüver in the USA initiated EAT (Experiments in Art and Technology), in which Robert Rauschenberg took part. If there is any continuation of this trend in Sweden at the moment, then the first name to occur in relation to it is Ulf Rollof (b. 1961), probably the young Swedish artist to have been given most media attention abroad in the past ten years, and one who took part in *documenta IX* in Kassel, Germany in 1993. He also featured in a solo exhibition arranged by Sweden's IASPIS at the Venice Biennale 1999.

Ulf Rollof. "Kylrock" (Cold mantle), 1989. Photo: P-A Allsten.
Collection Moderna Museet.

Ulf Rollof began his career as a photographer in the early 1980s. He investigates an abandoned building in central Stockholm. Later, while studying at the Royal University College of Fine Arts (1982–1987), he became an enthusiastic traveller, almost an explorer. In Mexico he finds both a culture and a natural world that fascinates him.

Survival is a central theme in Ulf Rollof's work. For instance, he took the name of the symbolic *Axolotl*, the fish which on rare occasions is transformed into a lizard, as the name of one of his exhibitions. And in Mexico he also encounters natural forces in a way that is decisive for his development as an artist and a human being, in the shape of the great earthquake in Mexico City in 1985. Rollof arrived there a few weeks after the catastrophe, and it is precisely catastrophe as a real event and a metaphor that is central to his work. "The catastrophe marks a point where it is no longer possible to carry on as usual. After the catastrophe, all at once the only thing that matters is keeping alive. No ordinary rules apply any longer ..." "In great natural catastrophes culture immediately becomes so tangible. At the same instant as the material network that bears up civilization is broken into pieces, the whole situation also becomes clear." In Mexico Rollof also came into contact with rubber production, which he studied in detail and later frequently returns to in his work.

Lifeboat was shown at Nordiskt Konstcentrum (the Nordic Arts Centre) in 1990. It is a work consisting of a large bellows pumping up another bellows in the shape of a boat or possibly a gigantic vagina. These two objects are communicating vessels that so to speak "breathe" together. Near them he placed 365 small lifeboats in synthetic wax, pigment, cotton and nylon, with latex-covered blackberries hanging along the railings as a kind of provisions. The third component of the installation comprised twelve wax paintings of calf foetuses that were illuminated from within (catastrophic in that they could not be born). The work was also shown at the Moderna Museet in the exhibition *Metafor och Materia* (Metaphor and Matter), 1991, and at the Biennale in São Paulo, Brazil, in the same year. At *documenta IX*, in 1993, Rollof exhibited a five-metre high bellows (*Bellows IX*) which is able to contract and lunge to catch flies which have been lured to it by the scent of manure and sugar. Red paintings were hung from the ceiling, however, to frighten off the insects. The gigantic sculpture was outwardly reminiscent of a huge fly. Rollof has subsequently become interested in developments in the former Soviet Union, and has among other things created a rotating Soviet star made of fir trees. He returned to the fir trees in a concept that related to air pollution and dying forests in the work he created with his daughter Sara for the *See how it feels* exhibition at the Rooseum in 1996.

Rollof has produced many sculptures with a powerful symbolic impact. Perhaps his *Kylrock* (Cold mantle), 1989, is particularly memorable. It is a military fur coat equipped with cooling tubes and a motor, a not especially far-fetched commentary on the earth's rising temperature—but he is never didactically officious, obvious or banal. Rollof is an enigmatic master of metaphor.

The works of sculptor Christian Partos (b. 1958) are characterized by passion and technology, combined with a passion for technology. They are often mobile, working with mobile light, and combine metal, water and video images, etc. They often involve existential motifs, and occasionally touch on Christian mysticism, as in his contribution to *Återkomster–nutida konst i Stockholms kyrkor* (Returning—contemporary art in Stockholm's churches) in 1995, *Lacrima Christi*. He created *Strålvispen* (Ray whisk) for the Swedish pavilion at Expo 2000 in Hannover. The work comprises five steel wires, each ten metres in length, with 1,000 individually switchable white light diodes. The wires rotate like giant skipping ropes

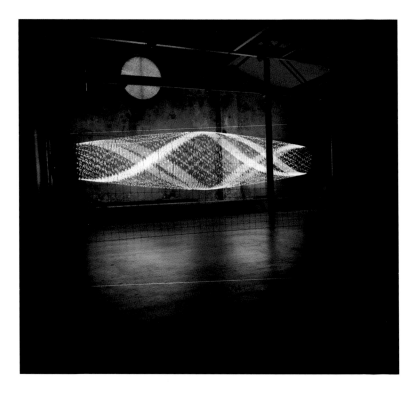

Christian Partos. "Strålvispen" (Ray whisk), Färgfabriken.
Photo: Stefan Frank Jensen.

and are controlled by a computer which creates animated patterns on the surface of rotation. In the following year the same work took pride of place in a magnificent show at Färgfabriken in Stockholm.

Add a dash of absurd humour to the concept of art & science, and the next destination becomes the duo of Bigert & Bergström (from 1986), consisting of Lars Bergström (b. 1962) and Mats Bigert (b. 1965). Their interest in science is marked by a fascination for history and culture. Bigert & Bergström appear to work in parallel with the biological implications of scientific experiments for humanity and the natural world and the cultural significance of visions as symbolic representations. At the same time their work fits in with the general picture of the postmodern situation with chilling precision. Nowhere in Bigert & Bergström's activities does reality stop to give any final answers. Neither is any order permitted to emerge that it might be possible to return to. All is movement and process. Their installations and constructions really deserve such fashionable designations as "projects" and "investigations".

"Wunderkammer"

The way in which B&B exhibit work, and never present a finished reality for viewers to observe but rather prepare an environment or an event (as in their performances) that requires the direct participation and interaction of the public, clearly distinguishes their activities from conventional museum exhibitions. In the historical background to their works they reveal a special interest in greenhouses, museums of natural history and biological dioramas (as exemplified by the Biological Museum in Stockholm). In terms of the history of art this opens a flood of associations to the forerunners of our present-day museums, the "Wunderkammer" (chambers of marvels) of Renaissance princes or other collections of curiosities and specimens of natural history—these, too, lacked the systematic approach with which our age organizes its museum collections for the archives. In the art-historical milieu of the twentieth century, the B&B duo might perhaps be regarded as latter-day relations of such surrealistically inclined artists as Joseph Cornell or Marcel Broodthaers. But B&B have nothing of their predecessors' social reticence. Their creative work is done centre-age, so to speak, in full public view. Like film-director and exhibition creator Peter Greenaway they problematize the would-be neutral interface of western museums

Bigert & Bergström. From "Klimatkamrarna" (Climate chambers—Incubator), 1995. Photo: Olof Wallgren, Swedish Travelling Exhibitions.

by involving the public in various events and exposing them to "forces that would normally be banned from the world of museums and galleries: vibrations, noise, heat, cold, wind ... neutral observation is rendered inoperable. Is it possible to get much further away from the 'white cube' of the traditional gallery than in *Klimatkamrarna* (Climate chambers), with their shifting physical sensations?" This work is the most consistent construction produced by Bigert & Bergström, and went on tour with *Riksutställningar* (Swedish Travelling Exhibitions) in 1993. The work is in six chambers: *Kuvös* (Incubator)—a protected environment, such as an indoor shopping centre or a scientist's trials in an experimental laboratory; *Värmekammare* (Hothouse)—nature itself is by no means "natural", but is dominated by cultural ideas: western Europeans long considered people in warmer countries to be "lazier" by reason of the climate (and developed this into the theories of eugenics); *Stormkammare* (Storm chamber)—on the poetically metaphorical force of the wind and its symbolic significance for the spirit; *Ljuskammare* (Chamber of light)—our age knows the heaven through the ozone hole and hell through nuclear power station meltdowns; *Ångkammare* (Steam chamber)—the greenhouse effect; and *Fryskammare* (Deep freeze chamber)—the dream of having yourself deep frozen to be awakened once the scientists of the future have made it possible ...

In addition to *Storm Chamber*, B&B have created a greenhouse with pulsating lungs for temporary exhibition at an underground station in Stockholm. In it they process the spiritual significance of the wind in a way reminiscent of the survival theme in Ulf Rollof's pneumatic bellows. These bellows too are interpreted against a background of the spark of life signified by respiration in our history of ideas (enthusiasm and inspiration are words based on the notion that God's spirit is injected into people, filling them with creative power). But where Rollof is the solitary traveller, a passionate, Romantic poet despite his scientism and his critique of civilization, a Tarkovsky of installation art, B&B are at the same time deeply committed on the issues of the environment and yet maintain an ironic distance. The *Climate chambers* (and several other works) have an element of parody in them with their citational technique and their light humour in relation to the shortcomings of science, but this does not diminish the seriousness of their endeavour. These characteristics do, however, place Bigert & Bergström firmly in a postmodern discourse, both in relation to the unfinished statement and their aesthetic stance with its many references to the domain of science.

Måns Wrange (b. 1961) goes much further in parodying the pretensions of science. His work often looks back to a Sweden about to disappear into history. Inventors and hobbyists give him ideas for objects and installations reminiscent of the land of childhood, such as a work with a spinning landscape and an immobile model railway, or reminiscent of the Swedish welfare state utopia, such as a table serving coffee in a decorative service, or reminiscent of our mental state, such as the so-called *Psychomobile*, powered by screaming your anxiety into a funnel. The on-going project *Misslyckandets encyklopedi*

Måns Wrange. "Psychomobile" (from the Encyclopedia of Failure), 1994.
Courtesy andréhn schiptjenko.

(Encyclopaedia of Failure), which has already gone through a number of chapters, is based on the fictive Professor Severin B Johansson's posthumous collection of investigations into such things as athletes who always finish in second place ... These investigations could never be completed, as the research work involved would then run the risk of proving a success, which would as it were contradict the fundamental point of the subject, which the professor came to embrace with increasing empathy over time. Wrange has continued his investigations, creating a project on the alternative *Indi* current, using a completely different system for measuring the value of work. He has also researched statistical material and created the Average Citizen Marianne. She lives alone in a two-room flat and has no children. But she has had a bust erected in her honour in the square outside the Magistrate's Court of Simrishamn in southern Sweden.

In his installations Henrik Håkansson (b. 1968) presents us with a completely different take on the collision between nature and culture. Originally, Håkansson was a photographer with a passionate interest in insects and other small creatures of the forests and the open countryside. He situates plants and animals—frogs, butterflies and grasshoppers, for instance—in the midst of the turbulence of pop culture. He installs frogs in discotheques with techno music throbbing in the semi-darkness under exotic plants and the speckled points of light from spinning mirror-surfaced globes, as in *FrogFor.e.s.t (eternal sonic trance)*, 1995. The exhibition was preceded by a rave party for tree frogs in a marsh in southern Sweden. Communication between human beings and animals has often had the poetic purpose of reconnecting us to something eternal and primitive. But Håkansson is rather trying to investigate our cultural habits, which have a colonizer's ambition where animals are concerned, that is to say, a desire to inscribe animals and plants into the human order of things.

Henrik Håkansson. FrogFor.e.s.t. (eternal sonic trance) Ecstatic Light, 1995.
Various Tree Frogs, Plants, Pool, Uva+b, Halogen lights, Timer, DJ turntable,
Fan Humidifier, Insects, Thermometer...
Courtesy Galleri Andreas Brändström.

"Viewing nature as something wild and primitive, something preceding culture, has more and more come to be replaced by a discussion turning on the insight that when humanity classifies things it 'creates' nature to the same extent that it creates us."

With great sensitivity Håkansson studied the butterfly population in Venice in preparation for his participation as Swedish representative in the Nordic pavilion of the Biennale of 1997. He collected caterpillars and set up a corner of the exhibition site for butterfly breeding, and even intended to reintroduce species that had become extinct in the region until it proved too difficult to realize. The butterflies appeared in multitudes, and he continued his investigations and classifications, on this occasion without the accompaniment of rock music.

Håkansson operates at the interface between the age's interests and its anxieties in the face of an ecological situation we have perhaps all too much influence on, a popular culture nobody can escape and a discussion about what is "natural" and how our relationship with the natural world is influenced by images of nature that form part of our cultural heritage. He does not moralize about this, but works with questions that arise spontaneously when these conflicting categories are brought together in one and the same exhibition. This creates a fertile environment where the question of the distinguishing quality of Swedish culture—often characterized as its closeness to the natural world—may be raised anew.

An open game with socially active players
This text about *artists in their rooms* has been arguing that there is a movement away from silent and empty exhibition rooms towards social spaces—hotels, supermarkets, the underground, shop windows, streets and public squares. Works have come to include video or film, sometimes dance

or other performance art, occasionally music or scientific strategies. Art, following this trajectory, is moving away from quiet contemplation towards reflection, whether this is reflection in the motif in an otherwise tranquil exhibition location or is an attempt to bring the viewer directly into the work by way of scenography or direct media interaction.

This argument is not particularly audacious. A glance at works that represent Swedish art abroad—whether by way of various cultural exchange programmes or at large-scale events such as the Venice Biennale or the Kassel *documenta* bears this out. And observers—curators, museum directors, critics— appear to be in full agreement about it. Which of course should lead us to expect that something radically different is waiting around the corner of the next century/millennium.

Matts Leiderstam (b. 1956) is a painter. In his painstakingly executed copies of old paintings he occasionally introduces a minor change which on closer examination proves to have altered things radically, or he might place the work so that it manifests a conscious relationship to its surroundings. In *Transpositions* (1998), new Swedish art presented in Cape Town, Leiderstam copied a 19th century painting, an equestrian motif that took on a faintly colonialist character in this context, which the staff of the South African National Gallery were hardly enthusiastic about exhibiting. A wealthy white bourgeois family on an excursion with the patriarch in the centre of attention. Minor shifts in the copy's reproduction of the original change the reciprocal relationships within the family. Here, as elsewhere in his work, there are allusions to homoeroticism. A homosexual himself, Leiderstam often works with the social complex of problems surrounding the subject. In one work for the *Moderna Museet Projekt*—the museum's contribution to a movement outside the institution towards other more openly social locations—he copied "Spring", by the 17th century French master Poussin.

The painting was then exhibited in an artificial concrete cave by a similarly artificial waterfall in a park in Paris, a much-frequented venue for cruising, the special gay mixture of strolling and picking up. Poussin's image of spring—a model for many 19th century city parks—was left to face the elements in the park, as a greeting from both the artist and art history. At one and the same time a commentary on dreams and reality, and on the passing of time. At the *Centre culturel suédois* (Swedish Cultural Centre) in Marais a photograph of the painting in the park was projected, and there was an open hole in the floor, a way out into the unknown…

Video is becoming more and more important. This medium, which has actually been in use for 40 years, if the 60s works of Korean-born Nam June Paik are taken as a starting point, won itself an undisputed position in the 1990s. This became clear at the Kassel *documenta X* in 1997 and at the Venice Biennale in 1999. In the Nordic countries, the Nordic Institute for Contemporary Art (Nifca), in collaboration with the exhibition *Nuit Blanche* at the Musée d'art moderne de la ville de Paris, organized a tour for video works and in September 1999, Moderna Museet staged a video festival for the youngest Nordic artists entitled *Blick* (gaze). The event was repeated in 2001.

The potential of video is great and still far from exhausted. From (often) being an idiosyncratic snatch of film shown on a monitor, video has grown by way of sculpture to installation, and in this way has often ended up shaping a whole room. A magnificent example at the 1999 Venice Biennale was *Electric Earth* by the American artist Doug Eitkens, which Lars O Ericsson in the daily *Dagens Nyheter* reviewed as "electronic blues presented in four specially built rooms with two wall-size projections in each".

Using the wall of a cleaners' store-room at a hotel, with 17 monitors distributed among the disinfectant, toilet paper and towels, Ann-Sofi Sidén (b. 1962) continues her single-minded voyage from works on the claustrophobic world of the paranoid psychiatrist Alice E Fabian to Dr Ruth Fielding's elaborate system of surveillance cameras. The work *Who Told the Chambermaid?*—exhibited at the Venice Biennale in 1999—allows us to follow from the secret hideaway of the cleaning closet the intrusion of surveillance cameras into a number of hotel rooms. The video is a mixture of authentic and staged scenes. The observer is left in doubt. "Is this an official registration of the hotel guests or a cleaner's rather obsessive pastime?", as Milou Allerholm asked in NU: .

In *Would a course of "Deprol" have saved van Gogh's ear?*—first exhibited at *Se hur det känns* (See how it feels) at the Rooseum in Malmö in 1996—she wallpapers a room with advertisements for feelgood pills and gives the room a door with no doorhandle. The observer is literally a captive of the scenography of the work. And in her contribution to the Moderna Museet's big show of Nordic art in 2000, *Organising Freedom*, the observer is drawn into a system of small rooms and booths, on the model of a porno club. This video installation, which is entitled *Warte mal!* (Wait a sec!), is a comprehensive documentation of the prostitution practised on the streets and in the cafes of the town of Dubi on the border between the Czech Republic and Germany. The work aroused great attention, as well it might, at her individual exhibition at the Musée d'art modern de la ville de Paris in the same year, and was later shown at the Hayward Gallery in London.

Miriam Bäckström (b. 1967) allows her public to be observers in a more conventional sense. She was also invited to the 1999 Venice Biennale by Harald Szeemann. She bases herself in a tradition of documentary photography, but at the same time appears to be seeking an atmosphere somewhere between cold reality and eerily lingering presence. By way of images from museum scenarios—preceded by film scenarios—her work is linked to the venerable task of photography not only to provide documentation but also to classify and index, to measure and evaluate what is depicted. She places, for instance, a picture from the Nordiska museet showing a tent, a temporary dwelling for a homeless person, which is now a museum exhibit and the object of a purchasing board's interest, next to an image from the IKEA museum in Älmhult, Småland, showing a typical 1960s interior. The photograph is authentic, the motif is manipulated—to appear "real". It is all a question of our collective memory. Miriam Bäckström previously produced a suite of pictures of the property of recently deceased people before their estate was dispersed. What presence does our self-suggestion persuade us to see in the absence shown in these images? The eye of the camera is neutral with respect to these questions, but still something personal, small-scale but powerful, steals into the unfeeling record made by the instrument. Museums wish to be a prop for our memory, but what these images tell us is not primarily *what* to remember, but much more what it *entails* to remember.

Magnus Wallin (b. 1965) has also enjoyed great success abroad—at the 2001 Venice Biennale, for instance—with his computer animated video art. A world of heat and cold and no mercy. *Exit* depicts an apocalyptic situation in which the crippled victims of war try to flee over an impassable obstacle, while *Skyline* shows athletic bodies flinging themselves into emptiness from the tower of the Olympic stadium in Berlin in 1936, to fall against the lower part of the tower, break into pieces and end up in the anatomical theatre of the 17th century scientist Olof Rudbeck at the University of Uppsala.

Art?

"What is Art?" is probably an eternal question. And although many contemporary artists say they are tired of it, a remarkably lively debate is still under way. It is naturally most vigorous in the field of idea-based art. Lars Vilks (b. 1946) wrote his PHD dissertation on the issue and summarizes laconically: "The *institutional theory of art* has conquered, and there is no option but to get used to it and come to terms with the artistic legacy in its light. It isn't easy, but I don't think there is any alternative. The answer to the question is thus that art is whatever we call art."

Vilks has been active as a concept artist since the mid-1970s. He used to be professor of the theory of art at the Royal University College of Fine Arts in Stockholm. His best known work is *Nimis*, constructed of flotsam and jetsam not far from the Kullen lighthouse on the West coast of Sweden. Both Nimis and the later stone sculptures *Arx* and *Omfalos*, next to it, have been criticized as illegal structures and form the object of ongoing legal actions which in the course of time have developed into a political performance. (*Omfalos* was removed by the authorities in December 2001). In the mid-1980s Nimis was sold for a symbolic sum to the German artist Joseph Beuys, one of Vilks's major sources of inspiration together with the American Robert Smithsom. Beuys died in 1986. Despite its isolated location, *Nimis* is indeed a social sculpture in the spirit of the master.

"A definition of art becomes old when you have at last managed to define it for yourself," declares Carl Michael von Hausswolf (b. 1960). He continues: "Art is also an excuse, a concept for something which cannot be categorized anywhere else. (…) You might say that Art forms a good host for parasites."

Unusually, von Hausswolff came to contemporary art via music. He mentions Karl-Heinz Stockhausen, Brian Eno, Pieter Brötzmann, Roxy Music and the "underground scene" in general as his sources of inspiration. He has made a number of CDs of electronic music, including one based on an electrical fault that is repeated again and again. More minimal than minimalism.

Magnus Wallin. "Exit", 1997. Moderna Museet.

With Leif Elggren (b. 1950), von Hausswolff founded the state of *Elgaland/Vargaland* (Elkland/Wolfland), which comprises all areas outside the territorial waters of existing countries and all border areas between different states together with various abstract and mental spaces. Their works often take the form of the ambassadors of this state.

The originators, of course, are serving ambassadors. At *documenta X* von Hausswolff contributed a work consisting of an electrified fence in the garden of the Ottoneum museum in Kassel. The transformer was on the upper floor of the building, between two windows giving on to the garden. The visitor could choose between either confronting the work in the garden and there experiencing how the fence crackled with electricity and gave off a techno-sound (like a kind of cattle fence), or from the window, where you could look down on the visitors in the garden and watch their reactions. At the

2001 Venice Biennale von Hausswolff and Elggren exhibited a sound sculpture in the Nordic Pavilion, a compilation of all the radio broadcasts that could be picked up at the location.

Sound art has taken its place on the current agenda, in fact. In June 2000 *Sonic Boom* was shown—and heard—at the Hayward Gallery in London, and in the autumn of 2001 the Swedish art magazine *Paletten* produced a thick issue solely devoted to the concept of sound art in conjunction with a number of performances and seminars that were being put on in Gothenburg. The same autumn, four seminars were held at the Moderna Museet to ring in sound in art in a broader sense. Thus the seminars took up art video, digital art, contemporary art music and sound art, together with performance. In all these disciplines sound is used. But of course the use of sound in art is older than this, from futuristic music to the radio drama of Öyvind Fahlström, from the experiments with light organs at the end of the 19th century to creaking mobile sculpture in the postwar period. *Fylkingen*, an association devoted to contemporary music and performance, has proud roots, particularly in the 1960s perhaps, when meetings were held at the Moderna Museet. The border between free contemporary art music and sound art is naturally elastic, but it is beyond dispute that art exhibitions today are no longer silent rooms but more and more tend not just to make a noise but also to develop into events. This is of course a development that sees its tradition as starting with the *happenings* of the 1960s. The historical consciousness of the younger generation is growing stronger and stronger in this field.

Video, performance and manipulated film images all form part of the arsenal when Tobias Bernstrup (b. 1970) and Palle Torsson (b. 1970) create their work. Both share an explicitly anti-elitist attitude with a powerful interest in the desires and dreams that popular culture—pop music, TV and pornography—try to satisfy. They collaborated to produce *A Museum*

Meltdown, a modified version of the computer game *Half-life* that has been shown at a number of museums, including the Moderna Museet in Stockholm. Here the visitor was able to grab a joystick in a small studio on the second floor and roam through a deserted museum on the first floor. Guards and monsters, *aliens*, pop up and you have to shoot your way past them and find your way through the museum collections. The philosopher and critic Sven-Olof Wallenstein develops an intelligent line of argument in relation to this in NU:, where he discusses the difference between *game* and *play*. The former is governed by rules, has a beginning and an end and may be controlled (if, that is, the rules are observed). *Play* also has certain rules, although they are less rigid, but no rule-book and no key. Here you are thrown into a play of drives and desires whose end no-one can foresee. The rules of the game are overthrown, the intruders are here, anything at all can happen. New rules cannot develop from the old ones. Here the concepts of both "art" and "museum" appear to be melting down.

Art appears to be heading towards a completely open pluralism in relation to style, technique and cross-disciplinary movement. The link between architecture and design was recently clearly demonstrated in the exhibition *What if— Art on the Verge of Architecture and Design—*, staged at the Moderna Museet in the summer of 2000. The 30 exhibitors— international artists and artistic groups—included such artists as Lotta Antonsson with her highly idiosyncratic fashion drawings, Miriam Bäckström with photographs of film sets, and Gunilla Klingberg (b. 1966) who exploded the logotypes of well-known brands and retail chains in expansive geometric patterns not unlike the flower power of the 60s.

Yet another tendency is represented by a reinvigorated painting movement. In the early autumn of 2001 Liljevalch's art gallery staged the exhibition *Vem är rädd för rött, gult och blått? Måleriet i förvandling* (Who's afraid of red, yellow and

Jacob Dahlgren. "Neither man nor nation can exist without a sublime idea, part II," 2002. Courtesy Galleri Charlotte Lund, Stockholm, wintergarten-kunst im raum, Vienna.

blue? Painting in transformation). Twelve young Swedish painters exhibited works with a striking wealth of invention and a voracious appetite for this traditional medium. They included Åsa Larsson (b. 1968), Jacob Dahlgren (b. 1970) and Linn Fernström (b. 1974). For a number of years Jens Fänge, too, (b. 1965) has been attracting attention for his delicate yet colourful painting using motifs which in a way are reminiscent of the hippy culture of the 1960s.

The 1960s is already passé as a retro-fashion. But the general fascination with the most myth-enshrouded decade of the 20th century endures.

The locations of art

At the *Skulptur* (Sculpture) exhibition at Kulturhuset in Stockholm in 1986, there was a glass door opening on to the street outside, an invitation to enter—and, particularly, to leave the room. The glass door had actually been designated a sculpture, and constituted Dan Wolgers' exhibit. One of many works by an artist who started his career as a maker of objects who was obsessed by inventiveness. Over time there were fewer and fewer objects and the ideas took on greater importance; the sculptor became a conceptualist, inspired not least by the American artist Chris Burden, the anonymous master of conceptual art of the 1970s.

An artist leaves the room, his work is a long farewell to the ego, to materials, to the room, to the institution ... The open glass door at Kulturhuset was followed in 1989 by self-portraits where the back of the head is turned to the viewer, also exhibited as part of the installation at the Venice Biennale, *Aperto*, in 1990. At the Liljevalch's Art Gallery, in the *Ecce homo* exhibition in 1992, he created his first "exstallation"—he quite simply removed two benches belonging to the gallery, took them to an auction firm and sold them. Partly, it is true, in revenge for the gallery stealing one of his ideas and using it for the exhibition poster without his permission, but also as a gesture of stepping out of a room, a central theme in Wolgers' work. He took the concept to its logical conclusion in 1991 by engaging an advertising agency to prepare and put on his exhibition at Galleri Bohman instead of doing it himself. The result was an exhibition of pop culture objects that

Dan Wolgers. "Här slutar allmän väg" (Public road ends here), 1995.
Courtesy Galleri Lars Bohman.

looked as if they wanted to be art. In 1992, in the Wanås palace grounds, he dumped rubbish from his studio in a heap and let the public salvage what it wanted and take it home. Everything went—but other rubbish was put there in its place! At the biennial in 1992, Wolgers exhibited nothing but the broken windows of the room he had been allocated (in an old industrial building). Once more the artist fled the room. Yet again he had bidden one of his many, long-drawn-out fare-wells.

In 1995 Wolgers exhibited objects such as photographs at Galleri Boman, the most controversial of which showed a large sign with the text: *Här slutar allmän väg* (Public road ends here). Precisely. Around the sign there is a garland of leaves as a frame, because frames are public. But the picture in the frame represents the artist himself—no public road—and the artist himself is also absent. This was also emphatically the case with a very controversial exhibition by Wolgers in 1991 at the same gallery, when he hired the design company Ri-fi-fi to create the exhibition for him.

It is evident that Dan Wolgers has a complex relationship not just to public spaces but also to exhibition rooms. This is not something he has stated explicitly himself, yet it is an almost unavoidable reflection if you consider his works over a period of time. But Wolgers is far from the only artist to bring the whole of the exhibition room, that is the whole frame, into his art. Though he seems to have got over this at least temporarily in the large exhibition at Liljevalchs Art Gallery in October 2001.

Fredrik Wretman manipulates the exhibition room as a whole by his habit of casting exhibition floors. At the same time, the viewer is shut out of the room and compelled to remain on the threshold. Wretman has occasionally made a comparison with the iconostasis of an Orthodox Christian church, but in fact no-one ever gets into a painting. Wretman's *American Floors* has already been mentioned (see page 78)—a brilliant idea using the exhibition area of a museum as the motif for an exhibition. Naturally, there are precedents, such as the Frenchman Yves Klein at Iris Clért's in Paris in 1957, who exhibited *Le Vide*, the emptiness. In the 1960s Robert Barry directed a more hard-boiled version by quite simply closing the gallery and leaving a note on the door for attendees on opening day: *during the exhibition the gallery will be closed*.

To a great extent the repudiation of the commercial parameters of art galleries in the 1970s led to art moving out into the streets and the countryside. In the USA, for instance, Robert Smithson worked with landscape art and Gordon Matta-Clark with the urban environment. These movements did not reach Sweden before Jan Håfström launched the *Ibid.* exhibitions (see page 130). Art's encounter with abandoned industrial premises resulted in a polyphony of utterances that emerged saturated with meanings from between the charged decay of the buildings and the seeking or provocative expression of the art. In 1976 Brian O'Doherty published the now-classic text *Inside the white cube*, which fixed this term for ever as the designation for the all-white exhibition room. When installation art came to be the dominant genre, which in Sweden's case can be said to take place around the latter half of the 1980s, artists consciously worked to extend their works to take in the whole exhibition space.

Among art locations that have made use of old industrial premises in Sweden, Läderfabriken (the leather factory) in Malmö may be highlighted. For a number of years in the late 1980s it hosted both studios and an exhibition area which became a vigorous free zone for experiments and a number of exhibitions by the young artists who rented studios on the premises. The Hårleman hall in Malmö was another industrial location used for exhibitions that attracted a lot of attention. Here installations in particular were exhibited for seven months in 1991. In Stockholm the Färgfabriken has successfully been implementing the same concept since 1995.

The rules of the game

But what happens when artists themselves organize an exhibition in public places? We have seen one answer in the remarkable *Spelets regler* (The rules of the game) exhibition that took place in the autumn of 1993 in central Stockholm.

On 14 March 1992 a frame of snooker balls was broken at Masters Billiard Hall at 6, Norrtullsgatan in Stockholm. Spheres knocked together, rolled apart and stopped. A map of Stockholm's city centre was unfolded beside them. A compass was used to ascertain the orientation of the table, after which the table and the balls were drawn on to the map in a thousandfold magnification. The original position of the white ball became the map's billiard saloon and its position after the break became the exhibition's information centre. Each

*of the fifteen artists had selected a ball, and was now bound
to the circle 57 metres in diameter that chance had allocated.
At the same time the exhibition area had been kept within
reasonable bounds.*

Artists Felix Gmelin (b. 1962) and Jörgen Gassilewski (b. 1961)
declare in the catalogue that *The rules of the game* is independent of the world of the galleries and institutions. The
requirement of precision in the total structure is emphasized:
"partly to motivate the statement that is always made by a
public presentation and partly because through its articulation
the exhibition creates a free space for the autonomy of the
work". In addition it was desired to "remove as many as possible of the hierarchies and categorizations that may ensnare
an observer". There is an awareness of the significance of context for art, but also a desire "to let the work of art decide for
itself and make precise its dependencies". "Autonomous art" is
among the most criticized phenomena of the age, on the
implicit assumption that no work can be "autonomous", that
is to say independent of its environment. But this catalogue
declaration indicates that the artists taking part are seeking a
condition resembling that of an autonomous state, that is they
are seeking independence, not isolation. They wish to make
the works of art visible, and "to help the work to sink its para-
sitical roots into place".

In *The rules of the game*, Dan Wolgers went into Odenplan
square in Stockholm and selected a person living in the vicin-
ity. He donated a collection of art (in which Wolgers was not
represented) to this individual and asked for it to be taken care
of. No conditions were made requiring public showing. Ann-
Sofi Sidén (b. 1962) showed great ethnological and archaeo-
logical enthusiasm in getting to the bottom of the city's not
particularly flattering legacy of old records from the seventeenth century, in which shaming punishments were inflicted

on women who had children out of wedlock. Anders Widoff's snooker ball stopped at a place corresponding to a post office—and as a result his work was sent off to a number of people, and individuals with postal giro accounts received a greeting from the artist. Jörgen A Svensson (b. 1958) demonstrated that art is communication, and established a coach link between Stockholm and Skoghall in Värmland in western Sweden. People from the country were able to travel to Stockholm and stay over Saturday night, while Stockholmers were compelled to stay in Värmland for a whole week, as the coaches only travelled on Saturdays. Charlotte Gyllenhammar created the most visible impact by hoisting an oak tree roots and all above Drottninggatan next to the Åhléns department store in the very centre of Stockholm (see page 45).

Public spaces ...

The randomness and contingency underlying this exhibition's method distinguishes it sharply from the approach of the National Arts Council. This is the institution which has hitherto located public works of art in official buildings and public spaces in Sweden. But as of 1998, its responsibilities have been extended and every public space has come within the purview of the Arts Council's interest and activities. The National Arts Council has been in existence since 1936, and has been working to get contemporary art into public view. The objective has been that one per cent of the construction cost of buildings intended for national and local government use should be spent on art. The most successful total solutions of the 1980s to the challenge of public art are Ulrik Samuelsson's magnificently theatrical scenography in the Kungsträdgården underground station and Sivert Lindblom's classical moulding of Blasieholmstorg square, both in the heart of Stockholm.

At the University College of Gävle-Sandviken in 1995, the

National Arts Council carried out a project with sculptures and installations by Ulf Rollof, Mikael Lundberg and Bianca Maria Barmen (b. 1960). It was presented as a series of encounters: between art and the environment, between different artists at this location and also between the artists and the users, that is to say those who will be living with the works of art on a daily basis. At this college Ulf Rollof has now installed sculptures of wolves moving in a path of chains over the glass wall of the main entrance. Mikael Lundberg has let an entropy series consisting of 41 pieces of safety glass, painted to a gradually increasing extent, cover an inside wall.

Ulrik Samuelsson. Kungsträdgården underground station at Arsenalsgatan exit, 1977. Photo: Hans Ekestang; courtesy SL.

Bianca Maria Barmen has placed her small, very distinctive, narrative bronze figurines in the external milieu of the college. The interplay in this college environment between art and architecture strives to establish dialogue in a kind of holistic concept—in contrast to the temporarily exhibited works of *The rules of the game* which do just the opposite, marking their independence of location even as they comment upon it. Of course these two exhibitions have different purposes, but even in relation to more official so-called off-art the advantages and disadvantages of temporary exhibitions are under discussion. In the summer of 1999, Annika Öhrner, who is on the board of the National Public Art Council (Statens konstråd), wrote an article in which she enumerated a considerable number of works of a temporary character. These included the relational aesthetics of works by such artists as Maria Lindberg and Elin Wikström.

and the Church ...

In recent years, contemporary art has returned to the Church in two projects. The first was *Skapelser* (Creations) in the summer of 1995, when almost 170 artists exhibited work in 26 churches in Götene, Lidköping, Mariestad and Skara in south-central Sweden. The second was *Återkomster* (Returns) in November, 1995, when 22 artists exhibited in 12 churches in the Stockholm area. The encounter between the location and the work of art is naturally highly charged in this context, but in almost all of the churches the work was seen through with interest and commitment from all those involved. In actual fact, few works were created to "fit in" with the setting, the commonest approach being independence and dialogue. As a contrast to these very spiritual exhibitions we may point to the installations carried out by a number of artists at the Malmborg ICA food market in Malmö in 1993, mentioned earlier in connection with Elin Wikström, an artist whose participation in this context may be considered as symptomatic as that of Jan Håfström at Engelbrekt Church in *Returns*.

Galleries—museums—art halls

A number of art museums and art halls in various parts of Sweden provide opportunities for showing new art, as do a large number of galleries, of which some are traditional in character—such as Aronowitsch, Nordenhake, Lars Bohman and others in Stockholm, Galleri Oijens, Mors Mössa and others in Gothenburg and Leger, Wallner and others in Malmö. Other galleries are run by artists' collectives like Konstakuten in Stockholm or have some other institutional character, like Forumgalleriet in Malmö with its links to the new college of art there, Forum. In Stockholm there is Galleri Mejan, where students of the Royal University College of Fine Arts (informally known as Mejan) are able to exhibit their work, while in Gothenburg Galleri Rotor is linked with the Valand College of Art. Other collective galleries in Stockholm are Enkehuset and Galleri Index. In the 1980s, Malmö had Läderfabriken and Gothenburg still has Konstepidemin, situated in the premises of the old isolation hospital, and Galleri 54 which is run by an artists' collective.

The Swedish Art Gallery Association *(Svenska Galleriförbundet)* was founded in 1986 and has 57 members (2002) from Ystad in the far south to Umeå on the northern coast of the Gulf of Bothnia. But in Stockholm alone there are well over a hundred art galleries.

Some of the private galleries, traditional in their commercial setup, have been more informal in their approach in the 1990s. After the financial collapse of the 1980s, a new generation of gallery owners took over in Stockholm, such as Andreas Brändström, who initially ran his gallery from his flat in Kungsholmen, later in an abandoned workshop in central Östermalm. Not too far from that is Galleri Roger Björkholmen, Galleri Schaper & Sundberg and Galleri Charlotte Lund. The initiative for *Smart Show* came from this circle of young gallery owners. This alternative art fair originated as a challenge to the more conventional Stockholm Art Fair, an art fair that has been held annually since 1980 at the north suburban Sollentuna Exhibition Centre. *Smart Show*, in its more informal way, had unconventional presentations of new art and also made use of the luxury passenger ferry Silja Symphony (1997) on the popular cruise route from Stockholm to Helsinki in Finland. As part of the same approach they have exhibited art at hotels, too, in both Stockholm and Gothenburg. (*Smart Show*, however, was later merged with the Stockholm Art Fair.)

The question of the locations of art is an appropriate

Ibid. II. The artists in front of the Ibid. II exhibition premises, 1983. (L to r), Sven Åsberg, Max Book, Johan Widén, Ola Billgren, Håkan Rehnberg (seated), Lars Olof Loeld, Lars Nilsson, Jan Håfström and Sivert Lindblom. Photo: Sven Åsberg.

Rooseum. Rooseum Center for Contemporary Art, Malmö. Photo: Per-Anders Jörgensen.

illustration of the movement of art in general over the past ten years, especially in Stockholm. Here the *Ibid.* exhibitions were emblematic for the early 1980s—atmospheric exhibitions, almost Gothic in their affinity for ruins, staged in silence in abandoned factory premises. *Ibid.* was the initiative of a group of artists led by Jan Håfström (mentioned above in the *The artists in the rooms* chapter), and there were two in Stockholm, a third in Borås, not far from Gothenburg. They became a kind of metaphor for an exploration of the layers of meaning in culture, language and art. In the cultural climate of the 1990s, surrounded by the incessant roar of the media, these silent rooms have been replaced by the much more social rooms found in hotels, for instance—corresponding to the social vitality and strong roots of new art in contemporary urban culture—in brief, the contextual range typical for the art that has emerged in the 1990s. At the same time, the galleries are finding their way to abandoned industrial premises. As for example the already mentioned Färgfabriken (the paint factory), located literally in an old paint factory in Liljeholmen on the outskirts of central Stockholm. It is a venture using both public and private sponsors with a broad range of art and culture, public meetings and debates. The interior of this building was perhaps expressed most beautifully in the autumn

1999 installation by Johanna Ekström (b. 1970) and Erik Pauser (b. 1957), *Brott* (Crime). Another striking industrial location is Magasin 3, which operates in warehouse 3 in Stockholm's freeport. After rebuilding in 2001 it is now larger than Malmö Art Gallery and as large as the old Moderna Museet. A considerable number of internationally renowned artists have shown their work at Magasin 3, including Gilbert & George, Chris Burden and Per Kirkeby. Skulpturens hus, the sculpture centre, was opened during Stockholm's European City of Culture year, 1998. It is located in a splendidly renovated cathedral of a factory, that used to make dynamite for Alfred Nobel, in Vinterviken in the suburb of Gröndal. Tensta art gallery is located in the north-western suburbs of Stockholm, in the centre of one of the most scathingly criticized housing estates created during what was known as the Million Houses Programme of the 1970s. It also opened in 1998, and has rapidly gained a solid reputation for relevant and timely exhibitions, often with international participation.

Art moving into premises built for other purposes has now become more of a rule than an exception. Splendid examples of conversion can be seen at the Rooseum in Malmö, the city's old electricity plant built in 1901 and renovated for use as an art hall in the 1980s by the financier Fredrik Roos, with the initial purpose of showing his own collection of Nordic and international art with its centre of gravity in the 1980s. The international collection was dispersed after his death in 1991, while the Nordic collection was kept intact as the joint property of the Rooseum and the Moderna Museet.

Malmö also has the Malmö Hall of Art (Malmö konsthall), which was opened in 1975 and contains one of the largest exhibition rooms in northern Europe. It can be arranged so that all the 2,225 square metres form a single open area. In the Malmö Museum of Art, located in the old Malmöhus fortress, there is a notable collection of Swedish and Nordic art of the twentieth century.

Röda sten is a new site for contemporary art and culture in Gothenburg located in an old heating central ("Pannhuset") under the Älvsborg bridge. The project started already in 1991 and events and exhibitions were held during the 1990s. After being renovated, Röda sten reopened in late spring 2000.

The Hasselblad Center is located in the Gothenburg Art Museum. Viktor Hasselblad, the creator of the famous Hasselblad camera, founded the centre. It opened in 1989 and moved into its new localities in 1996. The collection contains a growing number of international photography and focuses on Nordic works.

Nordiska Akvarellmuseet (the Nordic Water Colour Museum) is beautifully situated, practically on the water in Skärhamn on the island of Tjörn north of Gothenburg. The museum was inaugurated in June 2000 and specializes in water colour techniques in a broad meaning.

Among buildings which have received much attention in recent years we find the Sundsvall Museum/Kulturmagasinet (Culture Warehouse). Four blocks of food warehouses from the 1890s were converted into a unified complex to create a space for both permanent collections and temporary exhibitions, children's activities, a library and a cultural secretariat. The Kulturmagasinet was awarded the prestigious Europa Nostra prize in 1987 for the manner in which the restoration and conversion had been carried out. The Västernorrland Museum in Härnösand also deserves to be singled out for mention among newer museums in northern Sweden.

Among the private initiatives that have contributed to the showing of new art we may single out the exhibitions in the grounds of Wanås palace, near Kristianstad in Skåne, where after ten years of exhibitions a considerable collection remains on permanent display. Other examples are the art hall in

Hishult in Småland in the south-east and Umedalens Skulptur in Umeå in north-eastern Sweden. Forum in Stockholm is a cultural club on an intimate scale that puts on exhibitions of contemporary art, concerts, poetry readings, dance and theatre performances.

The Museum of Sketches (Skissernas Museum) in Lund forms part of Lund University. It is a specialized museum for the sketches and models of public and monumental works in Sweden. Over the years since its foundation in 1942, the museum has accumulated a unique collection of works.

Art education

The oldest kind of training for artists in the western tradition was a craft apprenticeship. When the first academies appeared in the sixteenth century, theories of art were developed that for a long time focused on the forms of nature in relation to those created by man. With the development of opposition to the academies (see below) came the movement that has hitherto dominated the art of the twentieth century—Modernism. Today our culture is confronted by an avalanche of images on an unprecedented scale, which has placed the concept of art in a new situation where it has become necessary to transcend modernism. In the absence of a better designation, our current position has come to be designated postmodern. This has been an analogical development to the designation of the industrial society in which modernism emerged as a post-industrial information society. The consequences for art education are a deeper awareness of the fact that no-one possesses the ultimate secret of how best to become an artist, or what an artist is, or what in fact art itself is. And yet the concept of art remains remarkably vital for both artists and the public, whether or not it is praised or attacked.

Art colleges in Sweden

In connection with the rebuilding of Stockholm's Royal Palace, which was initiated after the great Palace fire of 1697, Sweden obtained a Royal Academy of Draughtsmen in 1735. It was led by Guillaume Taraval, one of the nine artists imported from Paris to help work on the new Palace. In 1773, the Academy of Painters and Sculptors received its statutes from King Gustav III, providing the first opportunity for higher education—as this was understood at the time—for artists in Sweden. Gradually the Academy came to assume a position of total dominance. In the mid-nineteenth century discontent among certain artists provoked the *Opponent* movement into existence, and in 1886 this movement gave rise to the *Artists' Union*, which not only organized exhibitions in order to show other tendencies in art than those promoted by the Academy, but also provided tuition. The college of art in Gothenburg, Valand, was opened in the same year under the leadership of another of the Opponents, the painter Carl Larsson. Ever since, opinion regarding the Academy, from which the Royal University College of Fine Arts emerged, has oscillated for and against.

At present Sweden has five art colleges. Besides Stockholm and Gothenburg there are also colleges in Umeå and Malmö, while the University College of Arts, Crafts and Design, which opened in 1957 in Stockholm, is also recognized as an art college. During the 1990s, art colleges have undergone more or less radical changes. This is due to education now taking cognizance of the considerable changes that have occurred in art during the past four decades, especially in the 1990s. New art, a growing media market and new ways of producing art all demand a new approach to it. But this new approach should not be confused with a lack of principles or positions, for in fact, demands made on students have been made more precise, especially in relation to awareness of contemporary developments in the national and world community, of theory and of the knowledge needed of the practical aspects of showing art for those whose lives will depend on successful exhibitions. The professors are often artistic mentors for the young artists regardless of specialist demarcation lines relating to technique.

"The thought of an art college separate from the rest of the community seems as antiquated today as the image of the artist as a misunderstood genius, an unworldly bohemian with paint stains on his smock", writes the journal *Konstperspektiv* (Art perspectives) in a survey of Sweden's art colleges. And as if to echo this, Ann Edholm, an artist and professor at the University College of Fine Arts in Stockholm, declares: "As a young artist today you probably have to master a broader range than used to be the case, and you must be very active in making contacts. New tasks can include consulting commissions or working with companies or crossing the boundaries to other artistic areas such as film or scenography. The role of the artist has changed, and with it perhaps faith in art as such. It used to be something special to be an artist, but that has gone, you don't devote your life to the role of the romantic genius in the same way now." The University College of Fine Arts wants to help its students "find themselves", writes Professor Edholm, and concludes: "It always comes down to choice, whether you do the choosing yourself or someone else does it for you."

The Royal University College of Fine Arts in Stockholm
Students call it *Mejan*. The nickname derives from a count Meyer who in 1775 decided to donate a building to the Royal Swedish Academy of Fine Arts (Kungl Akademien för de fria konsterna) which was in acute need of premises. In 1908–09 the tuition became freer in relation to the Academy and was separated into a College of Fine Arts, (Kungl. Konsthögskolan) receiving its present name. The final separation from the Academy occurred at the end of the 1970s, and the Academy itself no longer offers any tuition. The teaching now takes place at new premises which were officially opened in 1995 on the islet of Skeppsholmen next to the new Moderna Museet and the Museum of Architecture. The old premises now con-

Students at the Royal University College of Fine Arts, Stockholm, 1997.
Photo: Tord Lund.

tain only the students' art gallery Mejan. The Academy owns the building, and both the exhibition rooms and the lecture hall may be hired. A new tenant, IASPIS (International Artists' Studio Programme in Sweden) has moved in, with guest studios and exhibition rooms. IASPIS extends invitations to Swedish and foreign artists to work in the premises, it arranges seminars and promotes international exchanges in other ways, too. The Academy building also houses exhibition premises for the General Association of Fine Arts (Sveriges Allmänna Konstförening) and Galerie Nordenhake (closed 2002).

The College has changed a good deal in recent years. The boundaries between its traditional departments have been erased. Its range of options now includes a five-year basic course in the fine arts, and programmes of architecture and restoration for a total of 230 study places. The goal of the Royal University College of Fine Arts is to provide tuition in both practical and theoretical topics, and the latter, too, are now compulsory. There are nine professors of fine art (including two guest professors), two professors of architecture, one professor of the theory of art and the history of ideas, and one professor specializing in photography, computers and video. There is also a tenured senior lecturer in the history of art. Variety is given priority, the broad modern concept of art is discussed and the college publishes a series of books with both classical and new theoretical texts in collaboration with a publishing company.

The University College of Arts, Crafts and Design in Stockholm

The University College of Arts, Crafts and Design (Konstfack) in Stockholm has its origins in a school of draughtmanship for craftsmen that was founded in Stockholm in 1844. From 1860 it was known as the Stockholm School of Handicraft and in 1878 it became the Technical College. It received its current designation in 1945. The College moved into its present premises on Valhallavägen, a stylistically pure specimen of 1950s functionalism, in 1959.

Teaching in fine art at the College currently includes programmes of painting, sculpture, photography, textile design and textile art. There is also a programme for video art and performance, and the College has just started a programme for exhibition curators. The duration of the programmes is from two years (curators, photography) to five years (painting). The University College of Arts, Crafts and Design also houses the Arts Education Institute, which trains Sweden's future art teachers. The subject *art* in Swedish schools is a kind of extended drawing course whose purpose is not just to teach children technical skills but also to provide them with an orientation in the image-laden world of contemporary art and media. The College has 600 places in all.

The University College of Arts, Crafts and Design has traditionally been a radical college with a high degree of contemporary awareness. The combination of educational opportunities for both free artists and for handicrafts professionals, designers and teachers makes this college a unique institution in Swedish art education. It is the combination of the college's qualities and the uncertainty as to what constitutes art and the insight that there is no "final word in the linguistic game that is art" which makes it especially relevant for the college to assume an attitude of sensitivity to contemporary currents, both theoretically and in practice. At the same time it proudly declares: "The college has not lost itself in specialization— *stucco lustro* is found right alongside seminars on Lacan".

The Valand Department of Fine Arts at Göteborg University
The Valand Department of Fine Arts at Göteborg University gets its name from the building of the same name into which it moved in 1886, 22 years after it was founded as Gothenburg's School of Museums and Drawing. Nowadays the college is located in a renovated building from the 1870s that was originally the Gothenburg School of Handicrafts (compare the origins of the University College of Arts, Crafts and Design in Stockholm). The strongly independent heritage at Valand has its roots in the individual chosen to run the school in 1886, Carl Larsson, who was a leading figure in the *Opponent* movement. There is a clear idea in Swedish art of a west coast school of painting, including the so-called Gothenburg colourists of the 1930s and 1940s, which has been an important factor in Valand's activities. It is worth mentioning a counter-weight in the central European influence exerted by the Hungarian immigrant Endres Nemes in the 1950s when he was running the college. Today it is emphasized that the tasks of art education are not regional but "national, if not international".

Valand. Graduation show at the Valand Department of Fine Arts at Göteborg University. Installation by Pia König, 1997. Courtesy Valand.

Given the general situation within the world of art, in which there is talk of an idea of art that is in dissolution or at the very least in a state of great change and extension, Valand is committed to "defending the room for art constituted by the studio". This idea gives rise to consideration for the student's self-awareness, which must of course also be reinforced by a heightened understanding of the context of art, that is to say the social situation within which the artist will have to work. This is a balance that all colleges of art have to take responsibility for, and in practice the point on the scale between individual and society at which the different colleges choose to locate themselves does not vary greatly.

In Gothenburg, too, there is a students' gallery, *Rotor*, where the students are able to exhibit their work as well as carry out projects which in addition to purely artistic aspects also involve practical and administrative training for a future independent career in art. The importance of artists contributing to a definition of themselves and their professional role in the community is emphasized by the school, but there is also a willingness to promote the more out-of-the-way, older painters who might tend to be neglected in the roar of the media. Valand has 60 students and a five-year programme of training.

Umeå University College of Fine Arts

Sweden's most northerly university is situated in Umeå. With it is associated the Bildmuseet (Image museum), and there are also two or three important galleries in the city. Sweden's fourth university college of art was started here in 1987, offering a five-year programme of training like the other colleges of art. It has 60 places and occupies the old Scharinska timber factory on the banks of the river Umeälven.

Like the other colleges of art, Umeå has the equipment to teach very diverse techniques, and similarly it has the ambition of helping students to attain a mix of personal development, technical skill, artistic realization, theoretical orientation and also training to meet various future practical and administrative challenges. However, the Umeå University College of Fine Arts appears to have a rather more informal style to its teaching, a special kind of playful approach which might be called investigative and exploratory in a very elemental sense. But then, comparisons with the seeking attitude of fundamental research are a frequent analogy in descriptions of contemporary art.

Network projects and other forms of collaboration have set their stamp on the College of Art in Umeå, which has been transformed quite significantly in the course of the past five years. International cooperation has taken off and the exchanges with artists in Los Angeles have influenced many of the college's students. The theoretical teaching has followed up this tendency. External examiners, such as Jan Hoet, the head of the museum in Ghent in Belgium and responsible for the *documenta IX* exhibition in Kassel, Germany, have contributed to the internationalization of the college.

Malmö Art Academy

The most recent addition to the Swedish colleges of art is Malmö Art Academy (Konsthögskolan i Malmö) at the University College in Malmö, which opened its doors on 1 July 1995. With funding from Lund University and with students from older schools of art in the city, Malmö Art Academy has a very international orientation and special emphasis on theoretical training, set courses and examination requirements that are more explicitly formulated than at any other college of art in Sweden in recent decades. The college also has its own gallery for students' work, Forum.

A concrete contribution to the college's international orientation is made by the funds earmarked for a special visiting professorship. Like Umeå, the college also makes use of foreign examiners. The degree programme lasts five years and totals 200 academic credits, of which half are awarded for individual independent work in the studios under staff supervision, and half are awarded for courses in artistic techniques, art theory and "projects of artistic realization led by internationally active artists". The range of options open to the students is so wide that in practice all students follow their own individual programmes. The college lays particular emphasis on encounters between people active within the contemporary art field, and with this in view organizes wide-ranging symposia. "The earliest academies," says Gertrud Sandqvist, the head of the college, "were not the closely regulated purveyors of art to the royal families of the seventeenth and eighteenth centuries, but the intimate and intense social gatherings of the Renaissance, where creators from the free arts intermingled."

And how do they make a living?

At the last count, in 1990, there were 21,149 artists in Sweden in the fields of image and form. 7,500 of them were registered in the appropriate artists' organizations. In addition there are many younger artists who do not belong to any artists' organization. The number of pictorial artists—painters, sculptors, photographers, etc—who were eligible for general artist's grants was estimated to be around 6,000.

These artists have an average annual income of some 98,500 kronor ($9,380), the lowest for any category of artists. Stage, music and literary artists all have a higher average income, even if it was still considerably less than the average Swedish income, which was around 150,000 to 200,000 kronor ($14,285-$19,047) in 1995. In addition, only a fifth of the incomes of pictorial artists derives from artistic work. The principal income of artists thus comes from doing bread and butter work on the side. It has been estimated that only a few hundred artists are able to live entirely by their art in Sweden today. To these we may add a few artists who receive a guaranteed income in the form of a central government artist's stipend.

Given this situation, how is it possible for so many young artists to work abroad? The answer, of course, is scholarships and grants of various shapes and sizes. A number of private funds and foundations contribute, but the most significant source is to be found in the means allocated annually by central government as display compensation for works in government possession, as these works are seen by the general public.

In 2001, this sum amounted to 61 million kronor ($5,809,523). This compensation is distributed by the Swedish Visual Artists' Fund in the form of project contributions and working scholarships. In large part this funding has made it possible for Swedish artists to live and work in Berlin, New York and San Francisco since the early 1980s. The 1990s trend towards bigger grants for fewer artists has considerably enhanced the reputation of young Swedish art abroad. And more and more young artists are making use of the opportunity. When the Moderna Museet opened its *On/About Time* exhibition in 1996, it transpired that a third of the artists invited were working abroad at the time (some of them more or less permanently). Some also find ways of remaining after their grants expire. The world of art is becoming more and more international.

Another—modest—source of income is the individual display compensation for artists that is collected by the copyright monitoring body "Bildkonst Upphovsrätt i Sverige" (Pictorial artists' copyright in Sweden). This body monitors the use of individual works in the press or advertising or in other ways. This support is individual, linked to the artist whose work is being used in such settings.

A government report into improving conditions for artists was published in January 1998. It proposes a substantial boosting of the opportunities of pictorial artists to work and to exhibit. It is proposed to redirect the financial support hitherto provided in the form of labour market measures to the sphere of cultural policy. This would reinforce the professionalism of artists and expand exhibition activities, thus making art more generally accessible. In 2001 an expert was commissioned to make a comprehensive study of the social security situation of artists and also of the way in which various subsidies, grants and other financial support affects the financial situation of artists in general. Artists in Sweden are hopefully on the threshold of a financial life that is both simpler and more secure. But there is good reason to anticipate that pictorial artists will still find it necessary to do a good deal of work on the side in the future, too, in jobs such as teaching.

Information about art

Sweden's deeply-rooted tradition of organized cultural activity has been of great significance in disseminating information about art. There are art societies at many big workplaces, and there are the more internationally familiar interest associations linked to certain halls of art and museums. The Swedish General Association of Fine Arts (*Sveriges allmänna konstförening, SAK*) was founded in 1886, but has its roots as far back as the 1830s. The Association publishes a yearly monograph about a Swedish artist and stages exhibitions at the Academy premises in Stockholm. There are associations of Friends of the Nationalmuseum, the Moderna Museet and Malmö Hall of Art, for instance, which also give important support in relation to purchases for these institutions. The National Federation of Art Associations in Sweden (*Sveriges konstföreningarnas riksförbund, SKR*) organizes a large number of societies throughout the country. In 2001, the Federation's own art journal—*Konstperspektiv* (Perspectives on art)—was transformed into an independent foundation. The Swedish Art Critics Association is an interest association for the country's art critics and the Swedish section of the international body Association Internationale des Critiques d'Art (AICA).

All the major daily newspapers in Sweden have an arts page with on-going coverage of art both in Sweden and abroad. Sweden also has a large number of cultural periodicals, of which a dozen or so are purely art journals.

Of course it is also possible to follow art developments in Sweden on the Internet. The site of art critic and IT consultant Anders Olofsson—*Konsten* (art), www.konsten.net—is an art magazine whose existence is entirely Net-bound. It features reviews of exhibitions as well as art books, a good archive and a lot of links to most aspects of the art scene in Sweden. Comprehensive information on Swedish culture is found at *Kulturnätet* (the culture net, www.kultur.nu). Although both of these sites are in Swedish, searching their links will take you to information on art in English. Certain daily newspapers and art magazines like *Paletten*, NU:, and *Glänta* also have websites with continually updated art coverage. Many artists have homepages of their own. Museums and exhibition halls have recently vastly expanded their Internet presence, providing discussion areas and other publicistic services. Problems remain, however, including such matters as image rights.

In a long-term perspective, regarding selectively targeted and interactive information about pictorial art, the Internet provides opportunities that would appear to be practically inexhaustible, even though they are of course strictly limited by the framework of the medium. But since Sweden has a leading position internationally in the use of computers by the general population, it is clearly possible that art information will not only be made available on the Net but also reach its intended public.

Epilogue

One autumn evening in the late 1990s, I ran into the painter Hans Wigert at Galleri Bohman in Stockholm. He has long been painting people and landscapes grounded in his own experience and in the restrained Swedish tradition that is at once lyrical and expressionist with roots that link back to the late 19th century. His painting contains no sign of being executed in this particular year, a mere two years away from a new millenium. And, naturally, Wigert is not alone in his approach. He may stand as a symbol for all the artists working in relative silence, known to the media and the art world, of course, and occasionally shown some interest, but never in the centre of attention. Perhaps they don't wish to be there, perhaps the atmosphere makes them uncomfortable. Perhaps they once received more attention, but now need to put some distance between themselves and what we call the contemporary scene.

This caveat pays muted homage to all those artists not included in this work. They have not set their stamp on the period—on the other hand, neither is their work stamped by the period. They are creative nonetheless—but at the moment others are more visible. Artists come and go, some find a place in the history books. Many of these "invisible" painters and sculptors nevertheless have a faithful public.

During the period dealt with in this account, art has incontrovertibly migrated from an empty room to a public one. But the whole of art cannot be captured in a single survey. And it is naturally quite appropriate to ask which art will be remembered in another time. Assuredly both that which is visible today and that which is not.

This survey started with a reflection on the way in which art has appeared to move from Picasso to Duchamp in the past 10–15 years, and the latter artist has an ambivalent remark relating to our final question about the fortunate artists who will make the history books:

"A good artist is just a lucky guy".

Sören Engblom
February 1998;
2nd revised edition, 2002

Footnote

The texts in this book are based on informal conversations with critics, artists and museum professionals, and on reviews and criticism published in the Swedish daily press and in specialist journals such as Beckerell (now defunct); Index and its predecessor Bildtidningen (especially in relation to photography; now defunct); Konstperspektiv; Konstvärlden; Material, 90-tal (now 00-tal); Paletten and Siksi (now NU:). Catalogues for the exhibitions referred to in the text have naturally been of great importance, as have Olle Granath's survey Ett annat ljus (Another Light, The Swedish Institute 1982), Carlssons, Stockholm, 1986; Swedish samples, A conversation on contemporary art, AICA Congress, Stockholm, 1994; Tankar om fotografi, ed. Jan-Erik Lundström, Alfabeta, Stockholm, 1993; Konstens anspråk (The claims of art), Lo Cajdal, production Glänta, Göteborg 1999; Sveriges Konst, 1900-talet, del III (Art in Sweden, 20th century, part III), Mårten Castenfors and the Swedish General Art Association (Sveriges Allmänna Konstförening) 2001; and my own publications such as From Interspaces and Broken Metaphors (Ed. For Art, Oslo), 1992 and the annual chronicles in the Bra Böcker/Focus Yearbooks 1990–95 (1996 CD-ROM, Norstedts).

A selection of Swedish art galleries and museums with modern art collections

Stockholm

Nationalmuseum
Fax +46 8 519 544 50   Tel. +46 8 519 543 00
www.nationalmuseum.se
Moderna Museet (Modern Museum)
Fax +46 8 519 552 10   Tel. +46 8 519 552 00
www.modernamuseet.se
Prins Eugens Waldemarsudde
Fax +46 8 667 74 59   Tel. +46 8 545 837 00
www.waldemarsudde.com
Thielska galleriet
Fax +46 8 446 72 41   Tel. +46 8 662 58 84
www.thielska-galleriet.a.se
Liljevalchs konsthall
Fax +46 8 508 313 26   Tel. +46 8 508 313 30
www.liljevalchs.com
Färgfabriken (Center for Contemporary Art and Architecture)
Fax +46 8 645 50 30   Tel. +46 8 645 07 07
www.fargfabriken.se
Magasin 3 Stockholm Konsthall
Fax +46 8 545 680 41   Tel. +46 8 545 680 40
www.magasin3.com
Skulpturens hus (The sculpture centre)
Fax +46 8 19 62 01   Tel. +46 8 19 62 00
www.skulpturenshus.se
Tensta Konsthall
Fax +46 8 36 07 63   Tel. +46 8 36 07 63
www.tenstakonsthall.com

Göteborg (Gothenburg)
Gothenburg Art Museum (Göteborgs konstmuseum)
Fax +46 31 18 41 19 Tel. +46 31 612 981 80
www.konstmuseum.goteborg.se
Röda sten
Tel./Fax +46 31 12 08 16
www.rodasten.com
Hasselblad Center
Fax +46 31 20 34 80 Tel. +46 31 20 35 30
www.hasselbladcenter.se

Skärhamn

Nordiska Akvarellmuseet (The Nordic Water Color Museum)

Fax +46 30 460 00 99   Tel. +46 30 460 80

www.akvarellmuseet.org

Malmö

Malmö Museum of Art (Malmö konstmuseum)

Fax +46 40 12 40 97   Tel. +46 40 34 10 00

www.malmo.se/konstmuseum

Malmö Hall of Art (Malmö konsthall)

Fax +46 40 30 15 07   Tel. +46 40 34 12 86

www.konsthall.malmo.se

Rooseum (Rooseum Center for Contemporary Art)

Fax +46 40 30 45 61   Tel. +46 40 12 17 16

www.rooseum.se

Lund

Museum of Sketches (Skissernas Museum)

Fax +46 46 222 49 81   Tel. +46 46 222 72

www.ldc.lu.se/skissernas/

Borås

Borås Konstmuseum

Fax +46 33 16 76 89   Tel. +46 33 35 76 71/72

www.boras.se/kultur/museer/konstmus/

Norrköping

Norrköpings Konstmuseum

Fax +46 11 13 58 97   Tel. +46 11 15 26 00

www.norrkoping.se/konstmuseet/

Sundsvall

Sundsvalls museum/Kulturmagasinet (Culture Warehouse)

Fax +46 60 61 58 94   Tel. +46 60 19 18 00

www.sundsvall.se/s-kommun/kultur/museum/

Umeå

BildMuseet

Fax +46 90 786 77 33   Tel. +46 90 786 52 27

www.umu.se/bildmuseet/

Mariefred

Grafikens Hus

Fax +46 159 231 70   Tel. +46 159 231 60

www.grafikenshus.se

Art colleges

Stockholm

Kungl Konsthögskolan (Royal University College of Fine Arts)
Fax +46 8 679 86 26   Tel. +46 8 614 40 00
www.kkh.se
Konstfack (University College of Arts, Crafts and Design)
Fax +46 8 783 05 63   Tel. +46 8 450 41 00
www.konstfack.se

Göteborg (Gothenburg)

Konsthögskolan Valand (Göteborg University, Dep. of Fine Arts, Valand)
Fax +46 31 773 51 19   Tel. +46 31 773 51 00
www.valand.gu.se
Högskolan för fotografi och film (School of Photography and Film at
Göteborg University,)
Fax +46 31 773 18 37   Tel. +46 31 773 18 31
www.foto.gu.se

Malmö

Konsthögskolan i Malmö (Malmö Art Academy)
Fax +46 40 32 57 05   Tel. +46 40 32 57 00
www.khm.lu.se

Umeå

Konsthögskolan (Umeå University College of Fine Arts)
Fax +46 90 786 66 87   Tel. +46 90 786 68 64
www.umu.se/art

Art magazines published in English

NU:
Jacobsgatan 27 nb
SE–111 52 Stockholm
Fax +46 8 402 3899   Tel. +46 8 402 38 90
www.nordicartreview.nu

Site
Minbyrån
111 49 Stockholm
e-mail: site@artnode.se

S.cr.a.m.
Kulturföreningen s.cr.a.m
Box 84
SE–240 13 Genarp

153

Index of names

THE SWEDISH INSTITUTE is a public agency established to disseminate knowledge abroad about Sweden's social and cultural life, to promote cultural and informational exchange with other countries and to contribute to increased international cooperation in the fields of education and research. The Swedish Institute produces a wide range of publications on many aspects of Swedish society. These publications can be obtained directly from the Swedish Institute or from the Swedish diplomatic missions abroad, and many are available on the Institute's website.

In the SWEDEN BOOKSHOP you will find—in many languages—books, brochures, fact sheets and richly illustrated gift books on Sweden, a broad selection of Swedish fiction and children's books, as well as Swedish language courses.

The Swedish Institute
Box 7434, SE-103 91 Stockholm, Sweden

Phone +46-8-789 20 00
Fax +46-8-20 72 48
E-mail si@si.se
Internet www.si.se   www.sweden.se